THE STORY
STUDY GUIDE

THE STORY

GETTING TO THE HEART OF GOD'S STORY

STUDY GUIDE | 31 SESSIONS

RANDY FRAZEE
WITH TOM ANTHONY

ZONDERVAN®

ZONDERVAN

The Story Study Guide
Copyright © 2016 by Randy Frazee

This title is also available as a Zondervan ebook.

Requests for information should be addressed to:
Zondervan, 3900 Sparks Dr. SE, Grand Rapids, Michigan 49546

ISBN: 978-0-310-08443-3

Interior design: Denise Froehlich

First Printing July 2016 / Printed in the United States of America

Contents

A Word from the Authors

As we journey through *The Story* in the days and weeks ahead, we will learn that heaven and earth are woven more closely together than we ever dreamed. All through the story of the Bible we see two parallel and beautiful dramas unfold.

There is the **Lower Story**. Humans live on earth and see things from a horizontal perspective. We can't see what is around the bend but must make a decision on which way to go, where we will live, and how we will respond to what happens to us. We focus on getting through the day as best we can. We interpret why we think other people do what they do. We struggle to know why certain things happen and why others things don't happen.

Then there is the **Upper Story**. This is how the story is unfolding from God's perspective—from above. Heaven is breaking into our world more than we recognize, and the story of God's seeking love, perpetual grace, and longing for relationship with ordinary people is breathtaking.

In the beginning of *The Story*, God walked with his first children in a beautiful garden ... in harmonious relationship. At the end of *The Story*, he will walk with us again, in a beautiful garden.

The question is: what will happen in the pages in between? As we walk through *The Story* together, we will see how God is weaving all of our Lower Stories to tell his one grand Upper Story.

Best of all, we can walk closely with him in every situation of life. As we recognize how close the Upper Story and the Lower Story fit together, we will learn to experience God's love and grace and be guided by his wisdom.

God wants to be with us; with you, with me. This is the refrain that rings true through *The Story*. As you read each chapter, this will become clearer and more personal and will fill your life with greater purpose, meaning, and understanding.

So, let God's Story become Your Story.

The Study Guide: Getting the Most from Your Journey

WITH GOD AND WITH OTHERS

The best ways for you to learn how the Upper Story and Lower Story are intertwined are to spend time seeking God on your own and to spend time seeking him with others. It's not an either/or. It's a both/and. *The Story Study Guide* is designed to help you spend important time each week with God and to help a biblical community seek God together. Using this study guide (and the related video) as tools for growth will help you fully embrace the Upper Story of God and your Lower Story role in his Upper Story.

SESSION OUTLINE

Each of the thirty-one sessions is divided into two parts. The first part, Personal Time, is for your own personal study, to be done prior to your group meetings. In this section you will *Know the Story* by reading one chapter from *The Story* and testing and expanding your Bible knowledge. You will *Understand the Story* by digging deeper into the passages. You will *Live the Story* by taking action on what you have learned. You will also *Tell the Story* by learning the five movements, discussing the chapter with those in your home, and praying together with those in your home. The Personal Time section can be completed in about one hour.

The second part of each session, Group Time, encourages you to seek God with others. You will *Know the Story* by sharing insights from your Personal Time. You will *Understand the Story* by using the note-taking outline to help you follow along with Randy Frazee's video teaching. You will *Live the Story* as you discuss your responses to several discussion questions and real-life scenarios of people who are growing in their faith. You will also *Tell the Story* as you use the movements to learn to tell the story together. The Group Time section can be completed in about one hour.

Finally, you will have the opportunity to pray for each other and for those not yet a part of your group. Use this section to record prayer requests to see how God works. Don't rush through or shorten this important part of developing the health of your group.

GROUP SIZE

The thirty-one-week *The Story* video curriculum is designed to be experienced in a group setting such as a Bible study, Sunday school class, or any small group gathering. To ensure everyone has enough time to participate in discussions, it is recommended that large groups watch the video together and then break up into smaller groups of four to six people for discussion.

MATERIALS NEEDED

Each participant should have his or her own study guide, which includes notes for video segments, memorization activities, and discussion questions. Simply coming to Group Time unprepared will still yield some benefit, but the maximum growth in your faith will occur as you engage *The Story* personally and with others in your home prior to meeting with your group. Although the course can be fully experienced with just the video and study guide, participants are also encouraged to have a copy of *The Story* book. Reading the book along with the full use of *The Story Study Guide* provides your best opportunity to make the journey richer and more meaningful.

FACILITATION

Each group should appoint a facilitator who is responsible for starting the video and for keeping track of time during discussions and activities. Facilitators may also read questions aloud and monitor discussions, prompting participants to respond and ensuring that everyone has the opportunity to participate. The best groups share the role of facilitator between several people over the course of the thirty-one weeks. Since some may be less comfortable in the role of facilitator, more thorough instructions are provided in the "Facilitator Tips for a Great Group" section that follows.

Group Time: Facilitator Tips for a Great Group

To ensure a successful group experience, read the following information before beginning.

—WHAT MAKES A GROUP DISCUSSION SUCCESSFUL?—

As a group's facilitator, you might be asking yourself, "What am I supposed to accomplish with this study?" Here are a few goals you might keep in mind for your group:

1. *Discovery.* The Bible is an amazing teacher. Don't underestimate the power of God as he reveals truth to those who read and discuss his Word. A successful group wrestles with Scripture in order to encourage these truths to come out.

2. *Relationship.* It takes time to develop meaningful relationships, but these relationships are incredible catalysts for spiritual growth. Encourage the group to share and enjoy building friendships. A successful group is more than just a Bible study.

3. *Authenticity.* Many people feel pressure to act "spiritual" when they are in religious environments, masking their true thoughts and feelings. This behavior stunts spiritual growth. Set the example for authenticity and honesty.

4. *Participation.* Groups that seek to include everyone in the conversation experience the most growth. Encourage the quieter members of the group with statements like, "Let's hear from someone who hasn't shared yet" or "Does anyone who hasn't shared yet have anything to add?" Successful groups engage all their members in their discussions.

At the end of each group meeting, ask yourself these questions: Did we learn something new about God and ourselves? Did we grow in our relationships with each other? Did we see honesty and authenticity in our discussion? Have we engaged all members of the group in the discussion? If you can answer yes to these questions, you are facilitating successfully.

CREATING A SUCCESSFUL ENVIRONMENT

Leading a group doesn't have to be overwhelming. Consider these tips to help you create a successful group environment:

Pray: As you prepare for your group meeting, ask God to give you wisdom in choosing discussion questions, courage in creating an authentic environment, and insight into the truths he wants to reveal to your group.

Prepare: Spend time before group preparing which sections of the study guide you will use and which questions work for your group. If you are struggling through the study guide and seem unprepared, people will feel more anxiety.

Prime: Your group will be as honest and authentic as you are willing to be. Courageously, set the tone for the group by being open about the strengths and weaknesses of your faith. You will prime the group by setting the example and letting them follow your lead.

Punctual: Start and stop on time. No matter how long your group meets, it's your job to keep things on track. Make a budget of time for each section of the study and stick to it. It might be uncomfortable to cut people off and move on, but the group will respect you for doing so.

SPECIFICS FOR THIS STUDY

Design your own discussion. You will not be able to use all of the group materials found in this study guide during the allotted time, so don't feel pressured to do so. Pick and choose the activities and questions that seem to fit your group the best.

Your group might gravitate to one or two of the discussion segments but not another; that's fine. Choose one or two questions from the segments that your group will benefit from most. Don't skip the section where people offer insights from their Personal Time. This will encourage them each week to study on their own ahead of your Group Time.

The case studies in every other session are based on actual situations. Use them as a creative vehicle to discuss the applications of the session's theme to real life.

Getting Started: The Heart of the Story and Our Story

Before the rise of the printing press in the sixteenth century, stories were passed down orally. The older people in a community shared the important stories of their history—all the principles and values of life woven within these gripping narratives. They shared these stories with each other, and with the next generation. It was a part of their culture ... their lives.

For the past few centuries, though, our communication primarily has been written—people sitting alone with a book open on their lap.

Now, however, with the explosive rise of technology (TV, movies, YouTube, and other visual communication tools), the world is returning to pictures and stories. We are once again becoming an oral culture. Indeed, many people learn best by hearing and telling stories.

With this in mind, we desire to capture this ancient/modern form of oral communication and weave it into your experience of *The Story*. To accomplish this, we have come up with five icons to help as you hear and tell the story. These simple pictures will put an image in your mind to help you remember the movements of God's story. They will also help as you tell your own story. Here are the images and the portion, or movement, of *The Story* that they represent:

Picture	Portion of The Story	Portion of the Bible
	The Story of the **Garden**	Genesis 1–11
	The Story of **Israel**	Genesis 12–Malachi
	The Story of **Jesus**	Matthew–John (Gospels)
	The Story of the **Church**	Acts–Jude
	The Story of a **New Garden**	Revelation

Over our thirty-one-week journey through *The Story*, we will spend a portion of both our Personal Time and Group Time focusing on one of these five movements, as indicated by the icon(s). Each one captures the Upper Story of God's work and also points to God's desire to encounter us in the Lower Story. Each session of your small group gathering will provide a brief time for your group to grow in your understanding of God's story as well as help you learn to articulate his story and your own journey of faith. Please don't skip this important part of the study.

Our prayer is that each person who walks through the thirty-one sessions of *The Story Study Guide* will be able to do three things.

1. Identify the five movements listed above and how they shape *The Story*.

2. Articulate a short statement that captures the heart of each of the five sections of *The Story* (see below).

3. Connect the themes of God's story with your personal story. This will release you to naturally tell your story of faith in a way that intertwines with God's story.

Here are the five movements of *The Story*. As you become familiar with the themes and reflect on how they connect to God's story, they will help you articulate your own story of faith.

Movement 1: The Story of the **Garden** (Genesis 1–11)

In the Upper Story, God creates the Lower Story. His vision is to come down and be with us in a beautiful garden. The first two people reject God's vision and are escorted from paradise. Their decision introduces sin into the human race and keeps us from community with God. At this moment God gives a promise and launches a plan to get us back. The rest of the Bible is God's story of how he kept that promise and made it possible for us to enter a loving relationship with him.

Movement 2: The Story of **Israel** (Genesis 12–Malachi)

God builds a brand-new nation called Israel. Through this nation, he will reveal his presence, power, and plan to get us back. Every story of Israel will point to the first coming of Jesus—the One who will provide the way back to God.

Movement 3: The Story of **Jesus** (Matthew–John)

Jesus left the Upper Story to come down into our Lower Story to be with us and to provide the way for us to be made right with God. Through faith in Christ's work on the cross, we can now overturn Adam's choice and have a personal relationship with God.

Movement 4: The Story of the **Church** (Acts–Jude)

Everyone who comes into a relationship with God through faith in Christ belongs to the new community God is building called the church. The church is commissioned to be the presence of Christ in the Lower Story—telling his story by the way we live and the words we speak. Every story of the church points people to the second coming of Christ, when he will return to restore God's original vision.

Movement 5: The Story of a **New Garden** (Revelation)

God will one day create a new earth and a new garden and once again come down to be with us. All who placed their faith in Christ in this life will be eternal residents in the life to come.

• • •

May this journey through *The Story* inspire you to share God's story freely, because he wants to make his story your story.

Creation: The Beginning of Life as We Know It

"In the beginning God created the heavens and the earth."

GENESIS 1:1

Creation	Noah and the Flood	Abram born

BC   2166

Personal Time

Every session in *The Story* contains a section for your Personal Time with God. This section is divided into four parts: Know the Story, Understand the Story, Live the Story, and finally Tell the Story, which is an opportunity to have a conversation about the chapter with those living in your home or with a friend. In total, the Personal Time section should take about one hour to complete, but you may want to use Tell the Story each day to help drive these truths deeper into your heart and life. Remember, there is no right or wrong way to do this. You are simply choosing a plan that fits you best as you try to embrace *The Story* in your life.

This week before your Group Time and your weekend worship experience, spend time using the Personal Time section of your study guide to allow the story of creation to take root in your heart.

KNOW THE STORY

Before reading Chapter 1 of *The Story*, answer the questions below to test your knowledge of this week's Scripture. Enter your answers in the column marked "1st Time."

Question	1st Time	2nd Time
1		
2		
3		
4		

1. Why did God create man in his image and likeness?
   a. He wanted us to be little gods.
   b. He wanted us to look like gods.
   c. He wanted us to have his character traits.
   d. He wanted us to rule over the creation.

2. Why did God banish Adam and Eve from the garden?
   a. God was angry with them.
   b. They had lost the privilege of the easy life.
   c. They could not be allowed to eat from the tree of life.
   d. God was trying to teach them a lesson about sin.

3. Why was God not pleased with Cain's offering?
   a. Cain did not do what was right.
   b. Abel had brought a better offering.
   c. God preferred an offering from the flocks.
   d. Cain's offering was too small.

4. Why did God send the flood?
   a. God regretted making human beings on the earth.
   b. God wanted to start over with Noah and his family.
   c. The human race had become evil.
   d. All of the above.

Now read Chapter 1 of *The Story*. After reading, revisit the questions to check your answers. Put your new answers in the column marked "2nd Time." (The answer key is found at the end of the session.)

UNDERSTAND THE STORY

As you read Chapter 1 of *The Story* during the week, allow the story of creation to help you see God's unchanging plan from the beginning.

1. Several verses begin simply with "God said." In what ways does this impact your view of God and his authority?

    _____
    _____
    _____
    _____

2. What do you think it means to be created "in the image of God"?

    _____
    _____
    _____
    _____

3. What led to the exile from the garden?

    _____
    _____
    _____
    _____

4. How does the rescue of Noah and his family along with the flood of the earth affect your understanding of the true nature of God?

    _____
    _____
    _____
    _____

5. After reading Chapter 1, what is one question you wish you could ask God about what you have read?

    _____
    _____
    _____
    _____

LIVE THE STORY

TAKE ACTION

We don't want to simply be hearers of the Word but also doers of the Word. Take some time to reflect on what you have read and studied this week.

1. Did you have a new discovery from your reading and study this week? If so, what was it?

_____

_____

_____

_____

_____

_____

2. Is there something you need to do based on what you learned?

_____

_____

_____

_____

_____

3. Who can you tell about what you learned? Make a plan right now to share with that person.

_____

_____

_____

_____

_____

_____

TELL THE STORY

As we go through *The Story* together, we want to learn how to tell the story. This week we will begin to focus on Movement 1. Read through Movement 1 below several times, beginning to commit it to memory.

🌳 Movement 1: The Story of the Garden (Genesis 1–11)

In the Upper Story, God creates the Lower Story. His vision is to come down and be with us in a beautiful garden. The first two people reject God's vision and are escorted from paradise. Their decision introduces sin into the human race and keeps us from community with God. At this moment God gives a promise and launches a plan to get us back. The rest of the Bible is God's story of how he kept that promise and made it possible for us to enter a loving relationship with him.

CONVERSATION

One day around a meal or your dinner table, have an intentional conversation about this week's topic. During the meal, read Genesis 1:1 found at the beginning of this session. Use the following question for discussion:

> Of all the things God has created, what is the one you find most interesting and why?

PRAY TOGETHER

Focusing the last thoughts of our day on God can help us rest — truly rest — in him. Each night read and reflect on Genesis 1:1, either on your own or with others if there are others living in your home. Pray and ask God to help you fully embrace the story of creation. As you do this each night before bed, let the power of the verse impact both heart and mind.

• • •

Group Time

Welcome .

Welcome to Session 1 of *The Story*. If this is your first meeting together, take some time to introduce yourselves and tell just a bit about how you came to be a part of this group.

KNOW THE STORY

Use one or both of these questions before you watch the video together.

1. How did you do on the quiz in the Know the Story section before you read the chapter?

    _____

    _____

    _____

2. What was your most interesting insight or question from your Personal Time this week?

    _____

    _____

    _____

UNDERSTAND THE STORY

As you watch the video for Session 1 of The Story, *use the section below to record some of the main points. (The answer key is found at the end of the session.)*

- The Bible is a _____ knitted together to tell the story of God's great love.

- What is the apple of God's eye? The magnum opus of his work? _____

- God took _____ with them in the cool of the day.

- God's Big Idea: The point of his story is to be _____ us!

- Every one of us is born with a _____ nature.

LIVE THE STORY

TAKE ACTION

1. What part of Randy's teaching encouraged or challenged you the most? Why?

2. Did anything from your Personal Time jump out, calling you to action? Did anyone have an "aha" moment?

CONVERSATION

Use one or two of the questions below (depending on time) to have a conversation in community.

1. What in the story of the garden gives you the most encouragement and why?

2. How does the story of Cain and Abel unsettle you or challenge you?

3. What hope and promise do you find in the story of Noah?

4. As you reflect on what you learned this week in Chapter 1, what is your biggest takeaway?

---------**TELL THE STORY**---------

As we go through *The Story* together, we want to learn how to tell the story. This week we will focus on Movement 1. Read it aloud together to start committing it to memory.

Movement 1: The Story of the Garden (Genesis 1–11)

In the Upper Story, God creates the Lower Story. His vision is to come down and be with us in a beautiful garden. The first two people reject God's vision and are escorted from paradise. Their decision introduces sin into the human race and keeps us from community with God. At this moment God gives a promise and launches a plan to get us back. The rest of the Bible is God's story of how he kept that promise and made it possible for us to enter a loving relationship with him.

---------**PRAY TOGETHER**---------

One of the most important things we can do together in community is to pray for each other. This is not simply a closing prayer to end Group Time but a portion of time to share prayer requests and life, to review how God has answered past prayers, and to actually pray for one another. Use the space below to record prayer requests and praises. Also, make sure to pray by name for people God might add to your group — especially your neighbors.

Name   *Request/Praise*

_____   _____

_____   _____

_____   _____

_____   _____

---------**NEXT WEEK**---------

Next week we'll look at the story of how of God's covenant promise with Abraham would accomplish his Upper Story plan through building the nation of Israel.

Know the Story Answer Key—d / c / a / d

Video Notes Answer Key—mural / people / walks / with / sin

God Builds a Nation

"I will establish my covenant as an
everlasting covenant between me and you
and your descendants after you for the
generations to come, to be your God and
the God of your descendants after you."

GENESIS 17:7

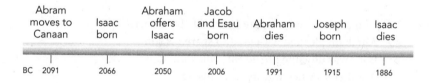

Abram moves to Canaan	Isaac born	Abraham offers Isaac	Jacob and Esau born	Abraham dies	Joseph born	Isaac dies
BC 2091	2066	2050	2006	1991	1915	1886

Personal Time

As noted last week, every session in *The Story* contains a section for your Personal Time with God. This section is divided into four parts: Know the Story, Understand the Story, Live the Story, and finally Tell the Story, which is an opportunity to have a conversation about the chapter with those living in your home or with a friend. In total, the Personal Time section should take about one hour to complete, but you may want to use Tell the Story each day to help drive these truths deeper into your heart and life. Remember, there is no right or wrong way to do this. You are simply choosing a plan that fits you best as you try to embrace *The Story* in your life.

This week before your Group Time and your weekend worship experience, spend time using the Personal Time section of your study guide to allow the story of Abraham and the beginning of the Hebrew nation to take root in your heart.

――――――――――**KNOW THE STORY**――――――――

Before reading Chapter 2 of *The Story*, answer the questions below to test your knowledge of this week's Scripture. Enter your answers in the column marked "1st Time."

Question	1st Time	2nd Time
1		
2		
3		
4		

1. What was the promise God gave to Abram?
    a. I will give you long life.
    b. I will give you countless offspring.
    c. I will give you great health.
    d. I will make you wealthy beyond measure

2. Why did God choose to spare Isaac's life from sacrifice?
    a. Abraham pleaded with God to spare his son.
    b. Isaac was unwilling to go through with it.
    c. Another sacrifice was made available.
    d. Abraham feared God.

3. When Jacob wrestled with the man through the night, what did he want from him?
    a. He wanted the man to simply let him go.
    b. He wanted the wealth the man possessed.
    c. He wanted a blessing from him.
    d. He wanted a promise of safety for his family.

4. Why did Jacob send flocks and herds to his brother Esau?
    a. He wanted to find favor in Esau's eyes.
    b. He knew Esau was in need.
    c. They were Esau's flocks and herds, and he was returning them.
    d. He didn't want to be a shepherd anymore.

Now read Chapter 2 of *The Story*. After reading, revisit the questions to check your answers. Put your new answers in the column marked "2nd Time." (The answer key is found at the end of the session.)

—UNDERSTAND THE STORY—

As you read Chapter 2 of *The Story* during the week, allow the story of Abraham and the beginning of the Israelite nation help you to see God's plan for his people.

1. If you were in Abram's sandals, what would be the biggest challenges of being asked to move to a new land?

2. What do you learn about God from the way he takes care of Hagar and Ishmael?

3. What is the most difficult thing for you to understand about the story of Abraham's sacrifice of Isaac?

4. Based on what you have read, how would you describe Jacob and why did you choose that description?

5. After reading Chapter 2, what is one question you wish you could ask God about what you have read?

_____

_____

_____

_____

_____

————————————LIVE THE STORY————————————

TAKE ACTION

We don't want to simply be hearers of the Word but also doers of the Word. Take some time to reflect on what you have read and studied this week.

1. Did you have a new discovery from your reading and study this week? If so, what was it?

_____

_____

_____

_____

2. Is there something you need to do based on what you learned?

_____

_____

_____

3. Who can you tell about what you learned? Make a plan right now to share with that person.

_____

_____

_____

TELL THE STORY

As we go through *The Story* together, we want to learn how to tell the story. This week we will continue our focus on Movement 1. Read through Movement 1 below several times as you continue to commit it to memory.

🌳 Movement 1: The Story of the Garden (Genesis 1–11)

In the Upper Story, God creates the Lower Story. His vision is to come down and be with us in a beautiful _____. The first two people reject God's vision and are escorted from paradise. Their decision introduces _____ into the human race and keeps us from community with God. At this moment God gives a promise and launches a plan to get us back. The rest of the Bible is God's story of how he kept that promise and made it possible for us to enter a loving relationship with him.

CONVERSATION

One day around a meal or your dinner table, have an intentional conversation about this week's topic. During the meal, read Genesis 17:7 found at the beginning of this session. Use the following question for discussion:

> What are some of the promises God has for us?

PRAY TOGETHER

Focusing the last thoughts of our day on God can help us rest — truly rest — in him. Each night read and reflect on Genesis 17:7, either on your own or with others if there are others living in your home. Pray and ask God to help you fully embrace the story of Abraham. As you do this each night before bed, let the power of the verse impact both heart and mind.

● ● ●

Group Time

Welcome

Welcome to Session 2 of *The Story*. If there are any new members in your group, take time for introductions. You might open your time with a brief prayer asking God to give you greater insights into his promises for us.

KNOW THE STORY

Use one or both of these questions before you watch the video together.

1. What surprised you from the quiz in the Know the Story section after you read the chapter?

   _____

   _____

   _____

2. What was your most interesting insight or question from your Personal Time this week?

   _____

   _____

   _____

UNDERSTAND THE STORY

As you watch the video for Session 2 of The Story, *use the section below to record some of the main points. (The answer key is found at the end of the session.)*

- A spiritual _____ was born in Adam and Eve.
- God thinks differently in the _____ story.
- They will see God as the one _____ the scenes of their lives.
- Abraham means father of _____.
- Moriah is the place that will later become the city of _____.

LIVE THE STORY

TAKE ACTION

1. What part of Randy's teaching encouraged or challenged you the most? Why?

2. Did anything from your Personal Time jump out, calling you to action? Did any part of your Personal Time call you to change something you were doing?

CONVERSATION

Have someone in your group read aloud the Case Study below and then discuss the questions that follow:

Maria was sharing with Karen about the difficult decision her family was facing. Maria and her husband, Marcus, were praying about whether or not to move to another city based on the great job offer Maria had received. So far, they didn't have clarity. Karen shared her perspective by saying, "If it were me, we would sit down and write out a list of all of the pros and cons of accepting the job and moving. Then, we would just look at which list was longer and stronger. I think God gives us clarity for direction by just using our own common sense."

1. If you were in Maria's shoes at this moment in the conversation, what are some of the things you would have to wrestle with as you prepared to respond?

2. Based on what you read and learned this week, how do you think Maria should respond to Karen's last statement?

---**TELL THE STORY**---

As we go through *The Story* together, we want to learn how to tell the story. This week we will continue our focus on Movement 1. Read it aloud together to continue to commit it to memory.

🌳 Movement 1: The Story of the Garden (Genesis 1–11)

In the Upper Story, God creates the Lower Story. His vision is to come down and be with us in a beautiful _____. The first two people reject God's vision and are escorted from paradise. Their decision introduces _____ into the human race and keeps us from community with God. At this moment God gives a promise and launches a plan to get us back. The rest of the Bible is God's story of how he kept that promise and made it possible for us to enter a loving relationship with him.

---**PRAY TOGETHER**---

One of the most important things we can do together in community is to pray for each other and those around us. Review your prayer requests from last week, and look for ways God has answered the prayers of your group. Then use the space below to record prayer requests and praises for this week. Also, make sure to pray by name for people God might add to your group—especially your neighbors.

Name   *Request/Praise*

_____   _____

_____   _____

_____   _____

_____   _____

---**NEXT WEEK**---

Next week we'll look at the incredible highs and lows of Joseph's Lower Story journey from slavery to second in command over all of Egypt.

Know the Story Answer Key—b / d / c / a

Video Notes Answer Key—virus / upper / above / many / Jerusalem

Joseph: From Slave to Deputy Pharaoh

"You intended to harm me, but God intended it for good to accomplish what is now being done, the saving of many lives."

GENESIS 50:20

Joseph sold into slavery	Jacob settles in Egypt	Jacob dies	Joseph dies
BC 1898	1876	1859	1805

Personal Time

Last week we looked at the story of Abraham and how God formed a nation through him. We also saw how the promises of God were so powerful in the life of Abraham and the nation of Israel.

This week before your Group Time and your weekend worship experience, spend time using the Personal Time section of your study guide to allow the story of Joseph to take root in your heart.

---------------------------KNOW THE STORY---------------------------

Before reading Chapter 3 of *The Story*, answer the questions below to test your knowledge of this week's Scripture. Enter your answers in the column marked "1st Time."

Question	1st Time	2nd Time
1		
2		
3		
4		

1. Why did Joseph's brothers want to get rid of him?
    a. Because of his coat of many colors.
    b. Because of his dreams.
    c. Because he was not a good shepherd.
    d. Because he cheated them.

2. What position of authority was Joseph given by Pharaoh?
    a. Joseph was made second in command in all of Egypt.
    b. Joseph was put in charge of the collection of grain.
    c. Joseph was put in charge of the distribution of food.
    d. All of the above.

3. When his brothers came to Egypt, what was Joseph's accusation against them?
    a. He accused them of being thieves.
    b. He accused them of being traitors.
    c. He accused them of being spies.
    d. He accused them of being murderers.

4. What was God's promise to Jacob in sending him down to Egypt?
    a. I will make you a great nation.
    b. I will give you plenty of food to eat.
    c. I will let you see your son before you die.
    d. I will let you see your great grandchildren.

Now read Chapter 3 of *The Story*. After reading, revisit the questions to check your answers. Put your new answers in the column marked "2nd Time." (The answer key is found at the end of the session.)

────UNDERSTAND THE STORY────

As you read Chapter 3 of *The Story* during the week, allow the story of Joseph to help you understand how God can work through difficult circumstances to bring about good.

1. What do you think was Joseph's mistake with his brothers? What advice would you have given him about how to handle his coat and his dreams?

    _____

    _____

    _____

    _____

2. Potiphar's wife falsely accused Joseph. Describe a time in your life you were falsely accused. What did you do? How did you handle it? If you could go back in time, what do you wish you could do differently?

    _____

    _____

    _____

    _____

3. What do we learn about God from the years of trials Joseph faced?

    _____

    _____

    _____

    _____

4. How did Joseph's understanding of what God was doing to save Israel in the Upper Story help him deal with what his brothers did in the Lower Story?

    _____

    _____

    _____

    _____

5. After reading Chapter 3, what is one question you wish you could ask God about what you have read?

_____

_____

_____

_____

———————————LIVE THE STORY———————————

TAKE ACTION

We don't want to simply be hearers of the Word but also doers of the Word. Take some time to reflect on what you have read and studied this week.

1. Did you have a new discovery from your reading and study this week? If so, what was it?

_____

_____

_____

_____

2. Is there something you need to do based on what you learned?

_____

_____

_____

_____

3. Who can you tell about what you learned? Make a plan right now to share with that person.

_____

_____

_____

_____

─────────────────────── TELL THE STORY ───────────────────────

As we go through *The Story* together, we are learning how to tell the story. This week we continue our focus on Movement 1. Read through Movement 1 below several times as you continue to commit it to memory.

🌳 Movement 1: The Story of the Garden (Genesis 1–11)

In the Upper Story, God creates the Lower Story. His vision is to come down and be with us in a beautiful _____. The first two people reject God's vision and are escorted from paradise. Their decision introduces _____ into the human race and keeps us from community with God. At this moment God gives a _____ and launches a plan to get us back. The rest of the Bible is God's story of how he kept that promise and made it possible for us to enter a loving _____ with him.

CONVERSATION

One day around a meal or your dinner table, have an intentional conversation about this week's topic. During the meal, read Genesis 50:20 found at the beginning of this session. Use the following question for discussion:

> What are examples of some of the good things God brings into our lives? How can things that first appear bad or negative turn out to be good or positive?

PRAY TOGETHER

Focusing the last thoughts of our day on God can help us rest — truly rest — in him. Each night read and reflect on Genesis 50:20, either on your own or with others if there are others living in your home. Pray and ask God to help you fully embrace the story of Joseph. As you do this each night before bed, let the power of the verse impact both heart and mind.

● ● ●

Group Time

Welcome

Welcome to Session 3 of *The Story*. If there are any new members in your group, take time for introductions. You might open with a brief prayer asking God to give you greater insights into Joseph's story.

KNOW THE STORY

Use one or both of these questions before you watch the video together.

1. How did you do on the quiz in the Know the Story section before you read the chapter?

   _____

   _____

2. What was your most interesting insight or question from your Personal Time this week?

   _____

   _____

UNDERSTAND THE STORY

As you watch the video for Session 3 of The Story, *use the section below to record some of the main points. (The answer key is found at the end of the session.)*

- Joseph was his dad's _____.

- The Lord was with Joseph so that he _____.

- God showed him _____ and granted him favor in the eyes of the prison warden.

- "It was to _____ lives that God sent me ahead of you."

- Let God _____ you during the difficult seasons to equip you for the assignment ahead.

LIVE THE STORY

TAKE ACTION

1. What part of Randy's teaching encouraged or challenged you the most? Why?

2. Did anything from your Personal Time jump out, calling you to action? Did anyone have an "aha" moment?

CONVERSATION

Use one or two of the questions below (depending on time) to have a conversation in community.

1. As you read the story of Joseph, what part was the most difficult for you to embrace? What part gave you the most encouragement?

2. Romans 8:28 says, *"And we know that in all things God works for the good of those who love him, who have been called according to his purpose."* How does the promise of this verse encourage you in some of your current circumstances?

3. How does Joseph's attitude toward his brothers challenge you in some of your own difficult relationships?

4. As you reflect on what you learned this week in Chapter 3, what is your biggest takeaway?

TELL THE STORY

As we go through *The Story* together, we are learning how to tell the story. This week we will continue our focus on Movement 1. Read it aloud together to continue to commit it to memory.

🌳 Movement 1: The Story of the Garden (Genesis 1–11)

In the Upper Story, God creates the Lower Story. His vision is to come down and be with us in a beautiful _____. The first two people reject God's vision and are escorted from paradise. Their decision introduces _____ into the human race and keeps us from community with God. At this moment God gives a _____ and launches a plan to get us back. The rest of the Bible is God's story of how he kept that promise and made it possible for us to enter a loving _____ with him.

PRAY TOGETHER

One of the most important things we can do together in community is to pray for each other and those around us. Review your prayer requests from last week, and look for ways God has answered the prayers of your group. Then use the space below to record prayer requests and praises for this week. Also, make sure to pray by name for people God might add to your group — especially your neighbors.

Name   *Request/Praise*

_____ _____

_____ _____

_____ _____

_____ _____

NEXT WEEK

Next week we'll look at the miraculous way the Lord delivered the Israelites out of bondage in Egypt.

Know the Story Answer Key — b / d / c / a

Video Notes Answer Key — favorite / prospered / kindness / save / mold

Deliverance

"Commemorate this day, the day you came out of Egypt, out of the land of slavery, because the LORD brought you out of it with a mighty hand."

EXODUS 13:3

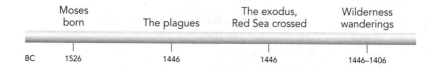

	Moses born	The plagues	The exodus, Red Sea crossed	Wilderness wanderings
BC	1526	1446	1446	1446–1406

Personal Time

Last week we looked at the story of Joseph and saw God take him through incredibly difficult circumstances into a life of blessing and reward.

This week before your Group Time and your weekend worship experience, spend time using the Personal Time section of your study guide to allow the story of the deliverance of the Israelites to take root in your heart.

---------------------------------**KNOW THE STORY**---------------------------------

Before reading Chapter 4 of *The Story*, answer the questions below to test your knowledge of this week's Scripture. Enter your answers in the column marked "1st Time."

Question	1st Time	2nd Time
1		
2		
3		
4		

1. Why did Pharaoh's daughter agree to keep Moses?
   a. She felt sorry for him.
   b. She was barren and wanted a child.
   c. She did not know he was a Hebrew child.
   d. She was trying to hide him from the public.

2. According to God, why did Pharaoh let the Hebrews go?
   a. Because of their growing numbers.
   b. Because of their military power.
   c. Because of God's mighty hand.
   d. Because of the plagues.

3. Why did Pharaoh change his mind and pursue the Israelites to the Red Sea?
   a. He was angry that they had escaped in the night.
   b. He was upset they had taken so much plunder from the Egyptians.
   c. He saw that the plagues had stopped.
   d. He was concerned the Egyptians had lost their free labor source.

4. If the people listened and kept God's commands, what did he promise to do?
   a. He promised to give them manna to eat.
   b. He promised they would not get any Egyptian diseases.
   c. He promised to provide quail for meat.
   d. He promised to provide water to drink from a rock.

Now read Chapter 4 of *The Story*. After reading, revisit the questions to check your answers. Put your new answers in the column marked "2nd Time." (The answer key is found at the end of the session.)

—————UNDERSTAND THE STORY—————

As you read Chapter 4 of *The Story* during the week, allow the story of the Israelites' deliverance help you see how God provides for and protects his people.

1. Put yourself in Moses's sandals. What would it have been like to be asked to take on such a big challenge from God? How do you think you would have responded?

_____

_____

_____

_____

2. What do you think was the purpose behind the plagues? How do the different plagues add to the power of the story?

_____

_____

_____

_____

3. How do you wrestle with the idea that it was God who hardened Pharaoh's heart? How does this affect your view of God? What other truths about God do you need to consider as you reflect on this?

_____

_____

_____

_____

4. What do you learn about the character and heart of God from his deliverance of the people of Israel and his provision in the desert?

_____

_____

_____

_____

5.   After reading Chapter 4, what is one question you wish you could ask God about what you have read?

_____

_____

_____

_____

——————LIVE THE STORY——————

TAKE ACTION

We don't want to simply be hearers of the Word but also doers of the Word. Take some time to reflect on what you have read and studied this week.

1.   Did you have a new discovery from your reading and study this week? If so, what was it?

_____

_____

_____

_____

2.   Is there something you need to do based on what you learned?

_____

_____

_____

_____

3.   Who can you tell about what you learned? Make a plan right now to share with that person.

_____

_____

_____

_____

TELL THE STORY

As we go through *The Story* together, we are learning how to tell the story. This week we continue our focus on Movement 1. Read through Movement 1 below several times as you continue to commit it to memory.

🌳 Movement 1: The Story of the Garden (Genesis 1–11)

In the _____ Story, God creates the Lower Story. His vision is to come down and be with us in a beautiful _____. The first two people reject God's vision and are escorted from _____. Their decision introduces _____ into the human race and keeps us from community with God. At this moment God gives a _____ and launches a plan to get us back. The rest of the Bible is God's story of how he kept that promise and made it possible for us to enter a loving _____ with him.

CONVERSATION

One day around a meal or your dinner table, have an intentional conversation about this week's topic. During the meal, read Exodus 13:3 found at the beginning of this session. Use the following question for discussion:

> What are some examples of how God has provided for us in big ways?

PRAY TOGETHER

Focusing the last thoughts of our day on God can help us rest — truly rest — in him. Each night read and reflect on Exodus 13:3, either on your own or with others if there are others living in your home. Pray and ask God to help you fully embrace the story of Israel's deliverance. As you do this each night before bed, let the power of the verse impact both heart and mind.

● ● ●

Group Time

Welcome

Welcome to Session 4 of *The Story*. If there are any new members in your group, take time for introductions. You might open with a brief prayer asking God to help you understand and embrace the story of the deliverance of the Israelites.

KNOW THE STORY

Use one or both of these questions before you watch the video together.

1. How did you do on the quiz in the Know the Story section before you read the chapter?

   _____

   _____

   _____

2. What was your most interesting insight or question from your Personal Time this week?

   _____

   _____

   _____

UNDERSTAND THE STORY

As you watch the video for Session 4 of The Story, *use the section below to record some of the main points. (The answer key is found at the end of the session.)*

- Moses said, "I am slow of speech and _____."

- In the Lower Story, Moses isn't _____ for such an important task.

- The best thing we can do is say "_____" to God.

- God has _____ on whom he wants to have _____.

- We will be saved by the blood of an _____ lamb.

LIVE THE STORY

TAKE ACTION

1. What part of Randy's teaching encouraged or challenged you the most? Why?

   _____

   _____

   _____

2. Did anything from your Personal Time jump out, calling you to action? Did anyone have an "aha" moment?

   _____

   _____

   _____

CONVERSATION

Have someone in your group read aloud the Case Study below and then discuss the questions that follow.

The two had barely sat down to dinner when Dwayne started describing challenges at work, so Mike just tried to listen. Messy office politics, a demanding boss, unreasonable deadlines, and limited pay increases were burying him. When their food arrived, the onslaught continued with Dwayne's issues at home, marriage tension, and financial burdens. Dessert shifted the talk to struggles with kids, arguments, and their choices of friends. Finally, Dwayne said, "We're thinking about just quitting, packing up the house and kids, and moving back to our hometown to start over."

1. Mike wants to provide godly counsel, but where do you think he should start?

2. Based on what you read and learned this week, what advice would you try to share with Dwayne if you were in Mike's shoes?

TELL THE STORY

As we go through *The Story* together, we are learning how to tell the story. This week we will continue our focus on Movement 1. Read it aloud together to continue to commit it to memory.

🌳 Movement 1: The Story of the Garden (Genesis 1–11)

In the _____ Story, God creates the Lower Story. His vision is to come down and be with us in a beautiful _____. The first two people reject God's vision and are escorted from _____. Their decision introduces _____ into the human race and keeps us from community with God. At this moment God gives a _____ and launches a plan to get us back. The rest of the Bible is God's story of how he kept that promise and made it possible for us to enter a loving _____ with him.

PRAY TOGETHER

One of the most important things we can do together in community is to pray for each other and those around us. Review your prayer requests from last week, and look for ways God has answered the prayers of your group. Then use the space below to record prayer requests and praises for this week. Also, make sure to pray by name for people God might add to your group — especially your neighbors.

Name *Request/Praise*

_____ _____

_____ _____

_____ _____

_____ _____

NEXT WEEK

Next week we'll look at the powerful commandments God gives to Moses and the Israelites and how he builds his Upper Story covenant with them.

Know the Story Answer Key — a / c / d / b

Video Notes Answer Key — tongue / qualified / yes / mercy / mercy / unblemished

New Commands and a New Covenant

"Then have them make a sanctuary for me, and I will dwell among them. Make this tabernacle and all its furnishings exactly like the pattern I will show you."

EXODUS 25:8–9

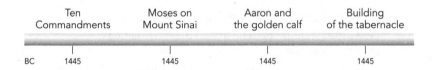

Ten Commandments	Moses on Mount Sinai	Aaron and the golden calf	Building of the tabernacle
BC 1445	1445	1445	1445

Personal Time

Last week we looked at the story of Moses and the deliverance of the Israelites from Egypt. Perhaps you were challenged to look at your own circumstances and watch for God's provision or protection in the midst of trials.

This week before your Group Time and your weekend worship experience, spend time using the Personal Time section of your study guide to allow the story of the commandments and God's covenant to take root in your heart.

—————————————————KNOW THE STORY—————————————————

Before reading Chapter 5 of *The Story*, answer the questions below to test your knowledge of this week's Scripture. Enter your answers in the column marked "1st Time."

Question	1st Time	2nd Time
1		
2		
3		
4		

1. Why did God want the people to hear him speaking to Moses from a dense cloud?
   a. God didn't want anyone to see him while he talked.
   b. God wanted to make sure the people heard him clearly.
   c. God didn't want Moses to have to remember everything he said.
   d. God wanted the people to always trust Moses.

2. Why did God command the people not to make an image or idol?
   a. God didn't want them to be like all the other nations.
   b. God is jealous.
   c. It was a reaction to the images and idols found back in Egypt.
   d. They did not yet have access to the right materials for proper idols.

3. Why did Aaron make a golden calf for the people?
   a. They wanted an idol like they had in Egypt.
   b. They were looking for a temporary distraction so they could have a party.
   c. Moses had been gone so long they didn't think he would return.
   d. Aaron was trying to take over leadership of the Israelites.

4. Why did Moses put a veil over his face when he talked to the Israelites?
   a. His face was radiant.
   b. He didn't want them to see his facial expressions.
   c. God told him to wear it as a sign of his leadership.
   d. It was the first of the priestly garments described by God.

Now read Chapter 5 of *The Story*. After reading, revisit the questions to check your answers. Put your new answers in the column marked "2nd Time." (The answer key is found at the end of the session.)

─────────────── UNDERSTAND THE STORY ───────────────

As you read Chapter 5 of *The Story* during the week, allow the story of the commandments and the covenant to help draw your heart closer to God.

1. Why did the people want to keep their distance from God? How do you see a similar response in the church today?

    _____

    _____

    _____

    _____

2. Of the Ten Commandments, which is the most challenging for you to keep and why?

    _____

    _____

    _____

    _____

3. What do you learn from the story of the golden calf?

    _____

    _____

    _____

    _____

4. What do you find most encouraging about God's interaction with Moses throughout this chapter? How would you say this fits into the Upper Story?

    _____

    _____

    _____

    _____

5. After reading Chapter 5, what is one question you wish you could ask God about what you have read?

_____

_____

_____

_____

_____

—LIVE THE STORY—

TAKE ACTION

We don't want to simply be hearers of the Word but also doers of the Word. Take some time to reflect on what you have read and studied this week.

1. Did you have a new discovery from your reading and study this week? If so, what was it?

_____

_____

_____

_____

2. Is there something you need to do based on what you learned?

_____

_____

_____

_____

3. Who can you tell about what you learned? Make a plan right now to share with that person.

_____

_____

_____

_____

TELL THE STORY

As we go through *The Story* together, we want to learn how to tell the story. This is our last week to focus on Movement 1. Read through Movement 1 below several times until you have it committed to memory. Then see if you can say all of Movement 1 without looking.

🌳 Movement 1: The Story of the Garden (Genesis 1–11)

In the _____ Story, God creates the Lower Story. His _____ is to come down and be with us in a beautiful _____. The first two people reject God's vision and are escorted from _____. Their decision introduces _____ into the human race and keeps us from community with God. At this moment God gives a _____ and launches a _____ to get us back. The rest of the Bible is God's story of how he kept that promise and made it possible for us to enter a loving _____ with him.

CONVERSATION

One day around a meal or your dinner table, have an intentional conversation about this week's topic. During the meal, read Exodus 25:8 – 9 found at the beginning of this session. Use the following question for discussion:

> What are some of the ways God dwells among us?

PRAY TOGETHER

Focusing the last thoughts of our day on God can help us rest — truly rest — in him. Each night read and reflect on Exodus 25:8 – 9, either on your own or with others if there are others living in your home. Pray and ask God to help you fully embrace the story of the commandments and the covenant. As you do this each night before bed, let the power of the verses impact both heart and mind.

● ● ●

Group Time

Welcome

Welcome to Session 5 of *The Story*. If there are any new members in your group, take time for introductions. You might open with a brief prayer asking God to help you understand and embrace the story of the new commands and covenant.

KNOW THE STORY

Use one or both of these questions before you watch the video together.

1. How did you do on the quiz in the Know the Story section before you read the chapter?

   _____

   _____

2. What was your most interesting insight or question from your Personal Time this week?

   _____

   _____

UNDERSTAND THE STORY

As you watch the video for Session 5 of The Story, *use the section below to record some of the main points. (The answer key is found at the end of the session.)*

- People see God as a cosmic _____.
- If I come down, there have to be _____ on how you treat me and how you treat each other.
- If I come down, I'll need a place to _____.
- If I come down, sin must be _____ for.
- And this new nation was to be _____.
- "If your _____ does not go with us, do not send us up from here."

---LIVE THE STORY---

TAKE ACTION

1. What part of Randy's teaching encouraged or challenged you the most? Why?

2. Did anything from your Personal Time jump out, calling you to action? Did anyone have an "aha" moment?

CONVERSATION

Use one or two of the questions below (depending on time) to have a conversation in community.

1. Based on Chapter 5, what do we learn about God's heart for his people and the motives behind his covenant with them?

2. In what ways do the Ten Commandments still guide your life today?

3. Put yourself in Moses's sandals in the Lower Story. What, to you, would be the most challenging part about his calling from God? What, to you, would be the best part?

4. As you reflect on what you learned this week in Chapter 5, what is your biggest takeaway?

TELL THE STORY

As we go through *The Story* together, we are learning how to tell the story. This is our last week to focus on Movement 1. Read it aloud together, and then see if you can all say it from memory.

Movement 1: The Story of the Garden (Genesis 1–11)

In the _____ Story, God creates the Lower Story. His _____ is to come down and be with us in a beautiful _____. The first two people reject God's vision and are escorted from _____. Their decision introduces _____ into the human race and keeps us from community with God. At this moment God gives a _____ and launches a _____ to get us back. The rest of the Bible is God's story of how he kept that promise and made it possible for us to enter a loving _____ with him.

PRAY TOGETHER

One of the most important things we can do together in community is to pray for each other and those around us. Review your prayer requests from last week, and look for ways God has answered the prayers of your group. Then use the space below to record prayer requests and praises for this week. Also, make sure to pray by name for people God might add to your group — especially your neighbors.

Name   *Request/Praise*

_____   _____

_____   _____

_____   _____

_____   _____

NEXT WEEK

Next week we'll look at the way the Lord miraculously provides for the Israelites as they wander in the desert for forty years.

Know the Story Answer Key — d / b / c / a

Video Notes Answer Key — killjoy / guidelines / stay / atoned / different / Presence

Wandering

"But Moses sought the favor of the LORD
his God. 'LORD,' he said, 'why should
your anger burn against your people,
whom you brought out of Egypt with
great power and with a mighty hand?'"

EXODUS 32:11

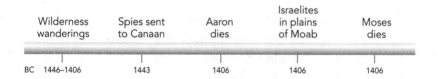

Wilderness wanderings	Spies sent to Canaan	Aaron dies	Israelites in plains of Moab	Moses dies
BC 1446–1406	1443	1406	1406	1406

Personal Time

Last week we looked at the story of Moses receiving the commandments and the covenant with God. Perhaps you were challenged to look closely at the Upper Story of God's desire to be in relationship with his people.

This week before your Group Time and your weekend worship experience, spend time using the Personal Time section of your study guide to allow the story of Moses and the Israelites wandering in the desert to take root in your heart.

---KNOW THE STORY---

Before reading Chapter 6 of *The Story*, answer the questions below to test your knowledge of this week's Scripture. Enter your answers in the column marked "1st Time."

Question	1st Time	2nd Time
1		
2		
3		
4		

1. Why did the Lord give the Israelites so much quail to eat?
   a. He knew they were starving in the desert.
   b. He knew the people had rejected him.
   c. He wanted to bless their obedience to him.
   d. He was displaying his power to the surrounding nations.

2. Why did Joshua and Caleb believe the Israelites could take the Promised Land?
   a. They believed the Israelite army was better trained.
   b. They believed they had the element of surprise.
   c. They believed the protection of the Canaanite people was gone.
   d. They believed they had superior numbers.

3. When Joshua was chosen to replace Moses, what spirit was recognized in him?
   a. He had a spirit of leadership.
   b. He had a spirit of humility.
   c. He had a spirit of wisdom.
   d. He had a spirit of inspiration.

4. Why did Moses challenge the people to choose life?
   a. They would then be able to love the Lord their God.
   b. They would then be able to listen to the voice of the Lord.
   c. They would then be able to hold fast to God.
   d. All of the above.

Now read Chapter 6 of *The Story*. After reading, revisit the questions to check your answers. Put your new answers in the column marked "2nd Time." (The answer key is found at the end of the session.)

UNDERSTAND THE STORY

As you read Chapter 6 of *The Story* during the week, allow the story of the wandering Israelites to help you understand God's love and protection despite their attitudes and actions.

1. What are some of the ways you see your own behaviors and attitudes in those of the Israelites?

2. Why do you think Caleb and Joshua were able to see things in a different light than the other ten spies?

3. Why do you believe Moses struck the rock at Meribah instead of obeying what God had asked him to do? Why was this so serious to God?

4. What are some of the miraculous ways you see God providing for his people, and what does this show you about the Upper Story?

5. After reading Chapter 6, what is one question you wish you could ask God about what you have read?

_____

_____

_____

_____

———————————————LIVE THE STORY———————————————

TAKE ACTION

We don't want to simply be hearers of the Word but also doers of the Word. Take some time to reflect on what you have read and studied this week.

1. Did you have a new discovery from your reading and study this week? If so, what was it?

_____

_____

_____

_____

2. Is there something you need to do based on what you learned?

_____

_____

_____

_____

3. Who can you tell about what you learned? Make a plan right now to share with that person.

_____

_____

_____

_____

TELL THE STORY

As we go through *The Story* together, we want to learn how to tell the story. This week we will begin to focus on Movement 2. Read Movement 2 below several times as you begin to commit it to memory.

 ## Movement 2: The Story of Israel (Genesis 12 – Malachi)

God builds a brand-new nation called Israel. Through this nation, he will reveal his presence, power, and plan to get us back. Every story of Israel will point to the first coming of Jesus — the One who will provide the way back to God.

CONVERSATION

One day around a meal or your dinner table, have an intentional conversation about this week's topic. During the meal, read Exodus 32:11 found at the beginning of this session. Use the following question for discussion:

> What are the things we know about God's heart for us—even when we do things that might make him unhappy?

PRAY TOGETHER

Focusing the last thoughts of our day on God can help us rest — truly rest — in him. Each night read and reflect on Exodus 32:11, either on your own or with others if there are others living in your home. Pray and ask God to help you fully embrace the story of the wandering Israelites. As you do this each night before bed, let the power of the verse impact both heart and mind.

● ● ●

Group Time

Welcome

Welcome to Session 6 of *The Story*. If there are any new members in your group, take time for introductions. You might open with a brief prayer asking God to help you understand and embrace the story of the wandering Israelites.

KNOW THE STORY

Use one or both of these questions before you watch the video together.

1. How did you do on the quiz in the Know the Story section before you read the chapter?

    _____

    _____

    _____

2. What was your most interesting insight or question from your Personal Time this week?

    _____

    _____

    _____

UNDERSTAND THE STORY

As you watch the video for Session 6 of The Story, *use the section below to record some of the main points. (The answer key is found at the end of the session.)*

- The second major problem with road trips is when the driver makes a _____ turn.
- The Israelites are heading to the fertile land of _____.
- The people decide not to move forward out of _____.
- They dragged their _____ into this mess as well.

- They have a fresh opportunity to _____ God.
- We would be _____ not to follow God's GPS.

LIVE THE STORY

TAKE ACTION

1. What part of Randy's teaching encouraged or challenged you the most? Why?

   _____

   _____

   _____

2. Did anything from your Personal Time jump out, calling you to action? Did anyone have an "aha" moment?

   _____

   _____

   _____

CONVERSATION

Have someone in your group read aloud the Case Study below and then discuss the questions that follow.

Many young women sought time with Sarah because she was so good at giving godly counsel. Allison was no different as she began to pour out her struggles. "Most days I wonder why I am stuck leading such a difficult team at work. We have a great company, and the future looks bright. We're well paid, and the work is rewarding. All day long, though, I hear complaints. My team grumbles constantly, always sees the glass half full, and can turn even good news into a crisis. They bicker and talk behind each other's backs. I go back and forth every day from wanting to lead them to a better future to wishing I could just fire them all tomorrow."

1. In what ways does this story parallel some of your own experience?

2. Based on what you read and learned this week, what type of godly counsel do you think Sarah will offer to Allison?

TELL THE STORY

As we go through *The Story* together, we want to learn how to tell the story. This week we will begin our focus on Movement 2. Read Movement 2 aloud together and begin to commit it to memory.

Movement 2: The Story of Israel (Genesis 12–Malachi)

God builds a brand-new nation called Israel. Through this nation, he will reveal his presence, power, and plan to get us back. Every story of Israel will point to the first coming of Jesus—the One who will provide the way back to God.

PRAY TOGETHER

One of the most important things we can do together in community is to pray for each other and those around us. Review your prayer requests from last week, and look for ways God has answered the prayers of your group. Then use the space below to record prayer requests and praises for this week. Also, make sure to pray by name for people God might add to your group—especially your neighbors.

Name   *Request/Praise*

_____   _____

_____   _____

_____   _____

_____   _____

NEXT WEEK

Next week we'll look at the how the Lord continues to unfold his Upper Story plan through Joshua and the Israelites entering the Promised Land in the Lower Story.

Know the Story Answer Key—b / c / a / d

Video Notes Answer Key—wrong / Canaan / fear / children / trust / fools

The Battle Begins

"Be strong and courageous. Do not be afraid;
do not be discouraged, for the LORD your
God will be with you wherever you go."

JOSHUA 1:9

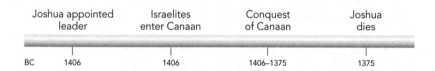

Joshua appointed leader	Israelites enter Canaan	Conquest of Canaan	Joshua dies
BC 1406	1406	1406–1375	1375

Personal Time

Last week we looked at the story of the wandering Israelites. Perhaps you were challenged in seeing how your heart toward God can affect generations to follow.

This week before your Group Time and your weekend worship experience, spend time using the Personal Time section of your study guide to allow the story of Joshua entering the Promised Land to take root in your heart.

KNOW THE STORY

Before reading Chapter 7 of *The Story*, answer the questions below to test your knowledge of this week's Scripture. Enter your answers in the column marked "1st Time."

Question	1st Time	2nd Time
1		
2		
3		
4		

1. Why had fear struck the hearts of the people of Rahab's city?
    a. They had heard the size of the Israelite army was a million men.
    b. They had heard the story of how the Israelites defeated Egypt.
    c. They had heard how God had dried up the Red Sea.
    d. They had heard stories of plagues coming on enemies of Israel.

2. What was the order of events at the battle of Jericho?
    a. March. Trumpets. Shout. Walls fall down.
    b. Trumpets. March. Shout. Walls fall down.
    c. March. Shout. Walls fall down. Trumpets.
    d. Trumpets. March. Walls fall down. Shout.

3. Why did the Israelites choose to defend the people of Gibeon?
    a. The Gibeonites had made a treaty with Joshua.
    b. The Gibeonites cried out to Joshua for help.
    c. Five kings had joined together to destroy Gibeon.
    d. All of the above.

4. Who did Joshua say would serve the Lord in his final words to the Israelites?
    a. Just himself.
    b. Himself and his household.
    c. Himself and his children's children to the fourth generation.
    d. All of the people of Israel.

Now read Chapter 7 of *The Story*. After reading, revisit the questions to check your answers. Put your new answers in the column marked "2nd Time." (The answer key is found at the end of the session.)

UNDERSTAND THE STORY

As you read Chapter 7 of *The Story* during the week, allow the story of Joshua to help you see the Upper Story of God's provision and protection for his people.

1. As Joshua prepared to enter the Promised Land, what are some of the reasons he may have needed to be challenged to be strong and courageous?

    _____

    _____

    _____

    _____

2. What, to you, is the most significant part of the story of Jericho, and why did you choose that part?

    _____

    _____

    _____

    _____

3. What are some of the ways God joined with Joshua in the battle against the Amorites?

    _____

    _____

    _____

    _____

4. As Joshua prepared to die, what do you think he was trying to accomplish in his final speech to the people?

    _____

    _____

    _____

    _____

5. After reading Chapter 7, what is one question you wish you could ask God about what you have read?

—————————————————**LIVE THE STORY**—————————————————

TAKE ACTION

We don't want to simply be hearers of the Word but also doers of the Word. Take some time to reflect on what you have read and studied this week.

1. Did you have a new discovery from your reading and study this week? If so, what was it?

---

2. Is there something you need to do based on what you learned?

---

3. Who can you tell about what you learned? Make a plan right now to share with that person.

TELL THE STORY

As we go through *The Story* together, we want to learn how to tell the story. This week we will continue to focus on Movement 2. Read Movement 2 several times as you continue to commit it to memory.

 Movement 2: The Story of Israel (Genesis 12 – Malachi)

God builds a brand-new nation called Israel. Through this nation, he will reveal his presence, _____, and plan to get us back. Every story of Israel will point to the first coming of Jesus — the One who will provide the _____ to God.

CONVERSATION

One day around a meal or your dinner table, have an intentional conversation about this week's topic. During the meal, read Joshua 1:9 found at the beginning of this session. Use the following question for discussion:

> What are some specific ways God might want us to show courage this week?

PRAY TOGETHER

Focusing the last thoughts of our day on God can help us rest — truly rest — in him. Each night read and reflect on Joshua 1:9, either on your own or with others if there are others living in your home. Pray and ask God to help you fully embrace the story of Joshua and his courage. As you do this each night before bed, let the power of the verse impact both heart and mind.

● ● ●

Group Time

Welcome

Welcome to Session 7 of *The Story*. If there are any new members in your group, take time for introductions. You might open with a brief prayer asking God to help you understand and embrace the story of Joshua.

KNOW THE STORY

Use one or both of these questions before you watch the video together.

1. How did you do on the quiz in the Know the Story section before you read the chapter?

   _____

   _____

   _____

2. What was your most interesting insight or question from your Personal Time this week?

   _____

   _____

   _____

UNDERSTAND THE STORY

As you watch the video for Session 7 of The Story, *use the section below to record some of the main points. (The answer key is found at the end of the session.)*

- The Upper Story plan of God must _____.
- Key Point: They needed to be people of the _____.
- Key Point: They needed to be people of _____.
- Key Point: They needed to be people _____ with God.
- In the Upper Story, God is bigger than the _____.

LIVE THE STORY

TAKE ACTION

1. What part of Randy's teaching encouraged or challenged you the most? Why?

   _____

   _____

2. Did anything from your Personal Time jump out, calling you to action? Did anyone have an "aha" moment?

   _____

   _____

CONVERSATION

Use one or two of the questions below (depending on time) to have a conversation in community.

1. In the story of Jericho — from Rahab to the final scene — what are ways you see the Lord directing the steps of the Israelites? What is he trying to show them?

   _____

   _____

2. In the midst of all the battles the Israelites faced in the Promised Land in the Lower Story, how would you summarize the Upper Story — God's overall story — for the book of Joshua?

   _____

   _____

3. As you read through Joshua's final words found on pages 100 – 101 of *The Story*, what part is the most challenging to you personally?

   _____

   _____

4. As you reflect on what you learned this week in Chapter 7, what is your biggest takeaway?

   _____

   _____

TELL THE STORY

As we go through *The Story* together, we want to learn how to tell the story. This week we will continue our focus on Movement 2. Read Movement 2 aloud together to continue to commit it to memory.

🕎 Movement 2: The Story of Israel (Genesis 12–Malachi)

God builds a brand-new nation called Israel. Through this nation, he will reveal his presence, _____, and plan to get us back. Every story of Israel will point to the first coming of Jesus — the One who will provide the _____ to God.

PRAY TOGETHER

One of the most important things we can do together in community is to pray for each other and those around us. Review your prayer requests from last week, and look for ways God has answered the prayers of your group. Then use the space below to record prayer requests and praises for this week. Also, make sure to pray by name for people God might add to your group — especially your neighbors.

Name   *Request/Praise*

_____   _____

_____   _____

_____   _____

_____   _____

NEXT WEEK

Next week we'll look at some of the heroes of Israel, including Deborah, Gideon, and Samson, as we see the Lord protect his people through judges in the Lower Story.

Know the Story Answer Key — c / a / d / b

Video Notes Answer Key — advance / Word / prayer / identified / giants

A Few Good Men ...
and Women

"How can I save Israel? My clan is the weakest in Manasseh, and I am the least in my family."

JUDGES 6:15

Judges begin to rule	Deborah's rule	Gideon's rule	Samson's rule
BC 1375	1209–1169	1162–1122	1075–1055

Personal Time

Last week we looked at the story of Joshua and the Israelites entering the Promised Land. Perhaps you were challenged to trust God to provide for you or protect you in the midst of difficult circumstances.

This week before your Group Time and your weekend worship experience, spend time using the Personal Time section of your study guide to allow the stories of the various judges to take root in your heart.

KNOW THE STORY

Before reading Chapter 8 of *The Story*, answer the questions below to test your knowledge of this week's Scripture. Enter your answers in the column marked "1st Time."

Question	1st Time	2nd Time
1		
2		
3		
4		

1. Why did Deborah tell Barak he would not receive honor in the battle with Sisera?
   a. Barak would only go to battle if Deborah went with him.
   b. The Lord had plans to deliver Sisera by the hand of a woman.
   c. Barak would not be able to defeat Sisera because Sisera was too powerful.
   d. All of the above.

2. What was the final thing encouraging Gideon to go into battle?
   a. The Lord gave Gideon two signs with the fleece.
   b. The Lord clearly chose the right soldiers to go into battle.
   c. Gideon heard the dream of a Midianite soldier.
   d. Gideon was told by an angel of the Lord the moment to attack.

3. Why did Samson finally tell his wife the answer to his riddle?
   a. She continued to press him for the answer.
   b. Samson was terrible at keeping secrets.
   c. She cried for seven days straight.
   d. She told him he didn't love her if he wouldn't tell her.

4. How was Samson able to get his revenge on the Philistines in the temple?
   a. His hair had grown back, and his strength had returned.
   b. He was placed in a strategic location in the temple.
   c. He prayed asking the Lord to strengthen him once more.
   d. All of the above.

Now read Chapter 8 of *The Story*. After reading, revisit the questions to check your answers. Put your new answers in the column marked "2nd Time." (The answer key is found at the end of the session.)

—UNDERSTAND THE STORY—

As you read Chapter 8 of *The Story* during the week, allow the story of the various judges to help you see the power, protection, and provision of the Lord in their lives.

1. In the story of Deborah, what is the relationship between the fortunes of the Israelites and their relationship with the Lord?

2. Based on how you saw Gideon use a fleece, how might you use fleeces in your own life when faced with challenging decisions?

3. As you read the story of Samson and Delilah, you see Samson edge closer and closer to revealing his secret. What does this show you about how temptation often works?

4. The story of Samson tells of a man with many flaws. How does his story challenge or encourage your understanding of the Upper Story of God?

5. After reading Chapter 8, what is one question you wish you could ask God about what you have read?

_____

_____

_____

_____

————————————LIVE THE STORY————————————

TAKE ACTION

We don't want to simply be hearers of the Word but also doers of the Word. Take some time to reflect on what you have read and studied this week.

1. Did you have a new discovery from your reading and study this week? If so, what was it?

_____

_____

_____

_____

2. Is there something you need to do based on what you learned?

_____

_____

_____

_____

3. Who can you tell about what you learned? Make a plan right now to share with that person.

_____

_____

_____

_____

---TELL THE STORY---

As we go through *The Story* together, we want to learn how to tell the story. This week we will continue to focus on Movement 2. Read Movement 2 below several times as you continue to commit it to memory.

Movement 2: The Story of Israel (Genesis 12–Malachi)

God builds a brand-new nation called _____. Through this nation, he will reveal his presence, _____, and plan to get us back. Every story of Israel will point to the first _____ of Jesus — the One who will provide the _____ to God.

CONVERSATION

One day around a meal or your dinner table, have an intentional conversation about this week's topic. During the meal, read Judges 6:15 found at the beginning of this session. Use the following question for discussion:

> What are different ways God can use small things and young people to help bless the world around us?

PRAY TOGETHER

Focusing the last thoughts of our day on God can help us rest — truly rest — in him. Each night read and reflect on Judges 6:15, either on your own or with others if there are others living in your home. Pray and ask God to help you fully embrace the story of Gideon's growing trust in God. As you do this each night before bed, let the power of the verse impact both heart and mind.

● ● ●

Group Time

Welcome

Welcome to Session 8 of *The Story*. If there are any new members in your group, take time for introductions. You might open with a brief prayer asking God to help you understand and embrace the stories of the judges in deeper ways.

—————————KNOW THE STORY—————————

Use one or both of these questions before you watch the video together.

1. How did you do on the quiz in the Know the Story section before you read the chapter?

    _____

    _____

    _____

2. What was your most interesting insight or question from your Personal Time this week?

    _____

    _____

    _____

—————————UNDERSTAND THE STORY—————————

As you watch the video for Session 8 of The Story, *use the section below to record some of the main points. (The answer key is found at the end of the session.)*

- "The LORD is with you, mighty _____."

- "This _____ will testify against them."

- Once delivered, the _____ will start all over again.

- God often chooses the most _____ candidate to accomplish his Upper Story plan.

- We think in the Lower Story God has _____ us, but his arms are wide open in the Upper Story.

---LIVE THE STORY---

TAKE ACTION

1. What part of Randy's teaching encouraged or challenged you the most? Why?

_____

_____

_____

2. Did anything from your Personal Time jump out, calling you to action? Did anyone have an "aha" moment?

_____

_____

_____

CONVERSATION

Have someone in your group read aloud the Case Study below and then discuss the questions that follow.

David and Sam were having their lunch break at work when Sam said, "That's easy for you to say. Everything always seems to work out in your life." As David started to respond, Sam jumped in again saying, "Look. You don't need to preach to me. I know I'm not doing everything God wants me to do. I know I need to get my act together so that I can get God's blessing. I know I need to go to church, read my Bible, pray, and get in a small group. It's my own fault, and I know I'm the one bringing these challenges on my family and me. I deserve to be judged, but I just can't seem to get my act together."

1. What parts of what Sam says resonate with the truth of the Bible? What parts don't resonate with the truth of the Bible? How do the Upper Story and the Lower Story work together in Sam's life and in the lives of others?

2. Based on what you read and learned this week, what should David say to Sam regarding what is actually the most important thing for him to do?

TELL THE STORY

As we go through *The Story* together, we want to learn how to tell the story. This week we will continue our focus on Movement 2. Read Movement 2 aloud together to continue to commit it to memory.

🕎 Movement 2: The Story of Israel (Genesis 12–Malachi)

God builds a brand-new nation called _____. Through this nation, he will reveal his presence, _____, and plan to get us back. Every story of Israel will point to the first _____ of Jesus—the One who will provide the _____ to God.

PRAY TOGETHER

One of the most important things we can do together in community is to pray for each other and those around us. Review your prayer requests from last week, and look for ways God has answered the prayers of your group. Then use the space below to record prayer requests and praises for this week. Also, make sure to pray by name for people God might add to your group—especially your neighbors.

Name   *Request/Praise*

_____   _____

_____   _____

_____   _____

_____   _____

NEXT WEEK

Next week we'll look at the story of Ruth and how the Lord uses her faithfulness and character to continue his Upper Story through the lineage of Jesus.

Know the Story Answer Key—a / c / a / d

Video Notes Answer Key—warrior / song / cycle / unlikely / abandoned

The Faith of a Foreign Woman

"Praise be to the LORD, who this day has not left you without a guardian-redeemer.... He will renew your life and sustain you in your old age. For your daughter-in-law, who loves you and who is better to you than seven sons, has given him birth."

RUTH 4:14–15

Time of the judges	Naomi and Ruth return from Moab	Ruth meets Boaz	Boaz marries Ruth

BC   1375–1050

Personal Time

Last week we looked at the stories of Deborah, Gideon, and Samson. Perhaps you were encouraged by the way the Lord accomplished his Upper Story plans through the lives of imperfect people.

This week before your Group Time and your weekend worship experience, spend time using the Personal Time section of your study guide to allow the story of Ruth to take root in your heart.

―――――――――――――**KNOW THE STORY**―――――――――――

Before reading Chapter 9 of *The Story*, answer the questions below to test your knowledge of this week's Scripture. Enter your answers in the column marked "1st Time."

Question	1st Time	2nd Time
1		
2		
3		
4		

1. What is Naomi's relationship to Ruth?
    a. She is her sister.
    b. She is her cousin.
    c. She is her mother-in-law.
    d. She is her friend.

2. Why did Naomi want her name changed to Mara?
    a. She had lost her husband.
    b. The Lord had made her life bitter.
    c. She had lost her sons.
    d. All of the above.

3. What was Ruth's reputation in town among the people?
    a. She was a woman of noble character.
    b. She was the poor widow who gleaned in Boaz's field.
    c. She was the young widow looking for a husband.
    d. She ran after the younger men in town.

4. When Boaz became Ruth's guardian-redeemer, what was his relationship to her?
    a. He became her legal guardian.
    b. He became her husband.
    c. He became her employer.
    d. He became her business partner.

Now read Chapter 9 of *The Story*. After reading, revisit the questions to check your answers. Put your new answers in the column marked "2nd Time." (The answer key is found at the end of the session.)

—UNDERSTAND THE STORY—

As you read Chapter 9 of *The Story* during the week, allow the story of Ruth to help you see how his Upper Story continues to unfold even in the midst of challenging Lower Story circumstances.

1. Early in the story of Ruth, what do you see in her and her character?

2. How is it tempting to be like Naomi when we face challenges in life?

3. The process by which Ruth presents herself to Boaz is foreign to us. What do you see in her actions that demonstrate having the right heart?

4. What are some of the noble steps Boaz takes as he walks through the process of becoming the guardian-redeemer? What are all the things he then receives?

5. After reading Chapter 9, what is one question you wish you could ask God about what you have read?

_____

_____

_____

_____

———————————LIVE THE STORY———————————

TAKE ACTION

We don't want to simply be hearers of the Word but also doers of the Word. Take some time to reflect on what you have read and studied this week.

1. Did you have a new discovery from your reading and study this week? If so, what was it?

_____

_____

_____

_____

2. Is there something you need to do based on what you learned?

_____

_____

_____

_____

3. Who can you tell about what you learned? Make a plan right now to share with that person.

_____

_____

_____

_____

TELL THE STORY

As we go through *The Story* together, we want to learn how to tell the story. This week we will continue to focus on Movement 2. Read Movement 2 below several times as you continue to commit it to memory.

🕎 Movement 2: The Story of Israel (Genesis 12 – Malachi)

_____ builds a brand-new nation called _____. Through this nation, he will reveal his presence, _____, and plan to get us back. Every story of _____ will point to the first _____ of Jesus — the One who will provide the _____ to God.

CONVERSATION

One day around a meal or your dinner table, have an intentional conversation about this week's topic. During the meal, read Ruth 4:14 – 15 found at the beginning of this session. Use the following question for discussion:

> How can we see God's fingerprints in some of the ways he provides for us?

PRAY TOGETHER

Focusing the last thoughts of our day on God can help us rest — truly rest — in him. Each night read and reflect on Ruth 4:14 – 15, either on your own or with others if there are others living in your home. Pray and ask God to help you fully embrace the story of Ruth. As you do this each night before bed, let the power of the verses impact both heart and mind.

● ● ●

Group Time

Welcome

Welcome to Session 9 of *The Story*. If there are any new members in your group, take time for introductions. You might open with a brief prayer asking God to help you understand and embrace the story of Ruth.

KNOW THE STORY

Use one or both of these questions before you watch the video together.

1. How did you do on the quiz in the Know the Story section before you read the chapter?

    _____

    _____

2. What was your most interesting insight or question from your Personal Time this week?

    _____

    _____

UNDERSTAND THE STORY

As you watch the video for Session 9 of The Story, *use the section below to record some of the main points. (The answer key is found at the end of the session.)*

- In the Lower Story, all is _____ for Naomi.
- "May the LORD _____ you for what you have done."
- Ruth was asking Boaz to be God's _____ to her.
- Boaz knew what it felt like to be an _____.
- Naomi means _____.

- In the Upper Story, God _____ their lives and accepts them as his own.

---------------**LIVE THE STORY**---------------

TAKE ACTION

1. What part of Randy's teaching encouraged or challenged you the most? Why?

2. Did anything from your Personal Time jump out, calling you to action? Did anyone have an "aha" moment?

CONVERSATION

Use one or two of the questions below (depending on time) to have a conversation in community.

1. Make a list of all of the examples of godly character depicted in the story of Ruth.

2. Now, make a list of all the ways you see God directing the story of Ruth. Look for examples where things were far more than simply coincidence.

3. As you look through the details of the Lower Story, how would you put the Upper Story of Ruth into one sentence or description?

4. As you reflect on what you learned this week in Chapter 9, what is your biggest takeaway?

TELL THE STORY

As we go through *The Story* together, we want to learn how to tell the story. This week we will continue our focus on Movement 2. Read Movement 2 aloud together to continue to commit it to memory.

🕎 Movement 2: The Story of Israel (Genesis 12 – Malachi)

_____ builds a brand-new nation called _____. Through this nation, he will reveal his presence, _____, and plan to get us back. Every story of _____ will point to the first _____ of Jesus — the One who will provide the _____ to God.

PRAY TOGETHER

One of the most important things we can do together in community is to pray for each other and those around us. Review your prayer requests from last week, and look for ways God has answered the prayers of your group. Then use the space below to record prayer requests and praises for this week. Also, make sure to pray by name for people God might add to your group — especially your neighbors.

Name   *Request/Praise*

_____   _____

_____   _____

_____   _____

_____   _____

NEXT WEEK

Next week we'll look at the stories of Samuel and Saul and how Saul begins with such promise but loses the Lord's blessing on his reign.

Know the Story Answer Key — c / d / a / b

Video Notes Answer Key — lost / repay / wings / outsider / beautiful / redeems

Standing Tall, Falling Hard

"For the foundations of the earth are
the LORD's; on them he has set the
world. He will guard the feet of his
faithful servants, but the wicked will be
silenced in the place of darkness."

1 SAMUEL 2:8–9

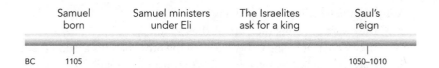

Samuel born	Samuel ministers under Eli	The Israelites ask for a king	Saul's reign
BC 1105			1050–1010

Personal Time

Last week we looked at the story of Ruth. Perhaps you were challenged to see how God directed the Lower Story steps of Ruth and Naomi to bring about his Upper Story plan for the line of Jesus to continue.

This week before your Group Time and your weekend worship experience, spend time using the Personal Time section of your study guide to allow the stories of Samuel and Saul to take root in your heart.

KNOW THE STORY

Before reading Chapter 10 of *The Story*, answer the questions below to test your knowledge of this week's Scripture. Enter your answers in the column marked "1st Time."

Question	1st Time	2nd Time
1		
2		
3		
4		

1. What did Eli tell the boy Samuel to say when he heard the voice in the night?
   a. "Speak, Lord, for your servant is listening."
   b. "Nothing can harm me while I am in the house of the Lord."
   c. "In the name of the Lord, I command you to leave this place."
   d. "If that is you, Lord, make yourself known to me."

2. Why did the Israelites ask for a king?
   a. They were rejecting the Lord as their king.
   b. They were just trying to be like all of the other nations around them.
   c. They were telling Samuel they didn't want Samuel's sons to rule them.
   d. All of the above.

3. How did Saul make his first public appearance as king over the Israelites?
   a. He met with a group of prophets and prophesied in front of all the people.
   b. He was chosen by Samuel as their king in the presence of all the people.
   c. He called men publicly to join him to rescue the people of Jabesh Gilead.
   d. He had a coronation ceremony where a crown was placed on his head.

4. What act caused the kingdom to be taken away from Saul?
   a. He lost a major battle with the Philistines at Mizpah.
   b. He had his kingdom taken away by the people of Israel.
   c. He offered a sacrifice himself instead of waiting for Samuel to do it.
   d. He blasphemed the Lord, and the Lord abandoned him.

Now read Chapter 10 of *The Story*. After reading, revisit the questions to check your answers. Put your new answers in the column marked "2nd Time." (The answer key is found at the end of the session.)

UNDERSTAND THE STORY

As you read Chapter 10 of *The Story* during the week, allow the stories of Samuel and Saul help you see the power of obedience and the consequences of disobedience.

1. As you look at Hannah's life over the years described, how do you see the Upper Story of God's blessing throughout the Lower Story ups and downs of her life?

2. What does the story of Samuel as a boy show us about his relationship with God?

3. What are all of the ways you see God orchestrating the process of choosing Saul as king?

4. What were the contributing factors to how things started so well with Saul and ended so poorly toward the end of his reign?

5. After reading Chapter 10, what is one question you wish you could ask God about what you have read?

_____

_____

_____

_____

LIVE THE STORY

TAKE ACTION

We don't want to simply be hearers of the Word but also doers of the Word. Take some time to reflect on what you have read and studied this week.

1. Did you have a new discovery from your reading and study this week? If so, what was it?

_____

_____

_____

_____

2. Is there something you need to do based on what you learned?

_____

_____

_____

_____

3. Who can you tell about what you learned? Make a plan right now to share with that person.

_____

_____

_____

_____

TELL THE STORY

As we go through *The Story* together, we want to learn how to tell the story. This is our last week to focus on Movement 2. Read Movement 2 below several times, filling in the blanks until you have it committed to memory. Then see if you can say all of Movement 2 without looking.

🕎 Movement 2: The Story of Israel (Genesis 12 – Malachi)

_____ builds a brand-new _____ called _____. Through this nation, he will reveal his presence, _____, and _____ to get us back. Every story of _____ will point to the first _____ of Jesus — the One who will provide the _____ to God.

CONVERSATION

One day around a meal or your dinner table, have an intentional conversation about this week's topic. During the meal, read 1 Samuel 2:8 – 9 found at the beginning of this session. Use the following question for discussion:

How does God guard our feet?

PRAY TOGETHER

Focusing the last thoughts of our day on God can help us rest — truly rest — in him. Each night read and reflect on 1 Samuel 2:8 – 9, either on your own or with others if there are others living in your home. Pray and ask God to help you fully embrace the stories of Samuel and Saul. As you do this each night before bed, let the power of the verses impact both heart and mind.

• • •

Group Time

Welcome

Welcome to Session 10 of *The Story*. If there are any new members in your group, take time for introductions. You might open with a brief prayer asking God to help you understand and embrace the stories of Samuel and Saul.

KNOW THE STORY

Use one or both of these questions before you watch the video together.

1. How did you do on the quiz in the Know the Story section before you read the chapter?

    _____

    _____

    _____

2. What was your most interesting insight or question from your Personal Time this week?

    _____

    _____

    _____

UNDERSTAND THE STORY

As you watch the video for Session 10 of The Story, *use the section below to record some of the main points. (The answer key is found at the end of the session.)*

- Samuel means "_____ by God."
- This is not the perfect will of God but rather his _____ will.
- The warning is, "You have to _____ God."
- Saul said he kept the best sheep to offer up a _____ to God.
- Israel had a _____ desire to be like everyone else.

LIVE THE STORY

TAKE ACTION

1. What part of Randy's teaching encouraged or challenged you the most? Why?

_____

_____

_____

2. Did anything from your Personal Time jump out, calling you to action? Did anyone have an "aha" moment?

_____

_____

_____

CONVERSATION

Have someone in your group read aloud the Case Study below and then discuss the questions that follow.

When Jen became a Christian, her life changed radically. She had not grown up in a Christian home, and she immediately jumped in with her entire heart. Her newfound faith affected her job, her home, her attitude, her friendships, her marriage, and her family. Over the years, though, she had begun to drift. She rarely read her Bible anymore. Her prayers had become a shopping list. Church attendance was consistent, but true involvement was sporadic. That early fire had dwindled to a flicker. Now her old friend Maggie was trying to figure out if there was any way to encourage her friend to rekindle the flame of faith.

1. What are specific ways you would encourage Maggie to pray before she ever approached Jen with words?

2. Based on what you read and learned this week, what specific words might provide encouragement to Jen? What words might provide a gentle warning?

TELL THE STORY

As we go through *The Story* together, we want to learn how to tell the story. This is our last week to focus on Movement 2. Read Movement 2 aloud together, filling in the blanks as you commit it memory. Then see if you can say it together as a group without looking.

Movement 2: The Story of Israel (Genesis 12–Malachi)

_____ builds a brand-new _____ called _____. Through this nation, he will reveal his presence, _____, and _____ to get us back. Every story of _____ will point to the first _____ of Jesus — the One who will provide the _____ to God.

PRAY TOGETHER

One of the most important things we can do together in community is to pray for each other and those around us. Review your prayer requests from last week, and look for ways God has answered the prayers of your group. Then use the space below to record prayer requests and praises for this week. Also, make sure to pray by name for people God might add to your group — especially your neighbors.

Name   *Request/Praise*

_____   _____

_____   _____

_____   _____

_____   _____

NEXT WEEK

Next week we'll look at the story of David and how the Lord takes a seemingly unimportant younger brother and raises him up to reign over all of Israel.

Know the Story Answer Key — a / d / b / c

Video Notes Answer Key — heard / permissible / follow / sacrifice / misplaced

From Shepherd to King

> "The LORD does not look at the things people look at. People look at the outward appearance, but the LORD looks at the heart."

1 SAMUEL 16:7

Samuel anoints David	David kills Goliath	Saul tries to kill David	Saul dies	David named king
BC 1025	1025		1010	1010

Personal Time

Last week we looked at the stories of Samuel and Saul. Perhaps you were blessed by the faithfulness of Samuel and challenged by Saul's gradual fall from power.

This week before your Group Time and your weekend worship experience, spend time using the Personal Time section of your study guide to allow the story of David being chosen as king to take root in your heart.

KNOW THE STORY

Before reading Chapter 11 of *The Story*, answer the questions below to test your knowledge of this week's Scripture. Enter your answers in the column marked "1st Time."

Question	1st Time	2nd Time
1		
2		
3		
4		

1. Why did David believe he had the earthly ability to defeat Goliath?
    a. He believed he was a mighty warrior.
    b. He knew he was a great shot with a sling.
    c. He knew he had already defeated a lion and a bear.
    d. He believed he was a lot stronger than all of his older brothers.

2. How did David go from being a hero to an enemy in Saul's eyes?
    a. The crowds cheered for David more than they cheered for Saul.
    b. David tried to take the kingdom away from Saul.
    c. David had several failures in battle, making Saul lose confidence.
    d. David did not treat Saul's daughter with favor.

3. How did Saul die in battle?
    a. A random arrow pierced his armor.
    b. He fell on his own sword.
    c. His armor bearer killed him when he was wounded.
    d. He was surrounded and struck by a spear.

4. What is the promise the Lord gives to David?
    a. I will give you peace from war for the remainder of your life.
    b. I will make you the wealthiest king on earth.
    c. I will give you more offspring than the sands on the seashore.
    d. I will establish your throne forever.

Now read Chapter 11 of *The Story*. After reading, revisit the questions to check your answers. Put your new answers in the column marked "2nd Time." (The answer key is found at the end of the session.)

UNDERSTAND THE STORY

As you read Chapter 11 of *The Story* during the week, allow the story of David to help you see how God sees our hearts.

1. What do you think the Lord was trying to show Samuel through the process of anointing David as king?

    _____

    _____

    _____

    _____

2. Write down a few of your main takeaways from the story of David and Goliath.

    _____

    _____

    _____

    _____

3. When David resisted the temptation to take Saul's life, what do we learn about his character and how he understood God's plans?

    _____

    _____

    _____

    _____

4. What were the things the Lord wanted to show David when David offered to build a temple for the Lord?

    _____

    _____

    _____

    _____

5. After reading Chapter 11, what is one question you wish you could ask God about what you have read?

_____

_____

_____

_____

_____

LIVE THE STORY

TAKE ACTION

We don't want to simply be hearers of the Word but also doers of the Word. Take some time to reflect on what you have read and studied this week.

1. Did you have a new discovery from your reading and study this week? If so, what was it?

_____

_____

_____

_____

2. Is there something you need to do based on what you learned?

_____

_____

_____

_____

3. Who can you tell about what you learned? Make a plan right now to share with that person.

_____

_____

_____

_____

TELL THE STORY

As we go through *The Story* together, we want to learn how to tell the story. This week we will begin to focus on Movement 3. Read Movement 3 below several times as you begin to commit it to memory.

Movement 3: The Story of Jesus (Matthew–John)

Jesus left the Upper Story to come down into our Lower Story to be with us and to provide the way for us to be made right with God. Through faith in Christ's work on the cross, we can now overturn Adam's choice and have a personal relationship with God.

CONVERSATION

One day around a meal or your dinner table, have an intentional conversation about this week's topic. During the meal, read 1 Samuel 16:7 found at the beginning of this session. Use the following questions for discussion:

> What does the world see in us when they only look at the outside?
> What does God see in us when he focuses on our hearts?

PRAY TOGETHER

Focusing the last thoughts of our day on God can help us rest — truly rest — in him. Each night read and reflect on 1 Samuel 16:7, either on your own or with others if there are others living in your home. Pray and ask God to help you fully embrace the story of David's rise from lowly shepherd to king of Israel. As you do this each night before bed, let the power of the verse impact both heart and mind.

● ● ●

Group Time

Welcome

Welcome to Session 11 of *The Story*. If there are any new members in your group, take time for introductions. You might open with a brief prayer asking God to help you understand and embrace the story of David's rise from lowly shepherd to king of Israel.

KNOW THE STORY

Use one or both of these questions before you watch the video together.

1. How did you do on the quiz in the Know the Story section before you read the chapter?

   _____

   _____

   _____

2. What was your most interesting insight or question from your Personal Time this week?

   _____

   _____

   _____

UNDERSTAND THE STORY

As you watch the video for Session 11 of The Story, *use the section below to record some of the main points. (The answer key is found at the end of the session.)*

- Saul was a five _____ king for sure.

- The Hebrew word to describe David is our English word:

  _____.

- "My God, my God, why have you _____ me?"

- Man looks at the outward appearance, but the Lord looks at the

  _____.

- And David _____ them with integrity of heart.
- David was the _____ in the Lower Story.

———————————**LIVE THE STORY**———————————

TAKE ACTION

1. What part of Randy's teaching encouraged or challenged you the most? Why?

    _____

    _____

    _____

2. Did anything from your Personal Time jump out, calling you to action? Did anyone have an "aha" moment?

    _____

    _____

    _____

CONVERSATION

Use one or two of the questions below (depending on time) to have a conversation in community.

1. What do we learn about God through the story of David and Goliath? What do we learn about David from this story?

    _____

    _____

    _____

    _____

2. As you put yourself in David's sandals, how would you have struggled with waiting on God during the years between his anointing and Saul's eventual death?

    _____

    _____

    _____

    _____

3. What do you see in the final promise God gave to David (the promise of his throne being established forever)? How do you think he would have seen this blessing in light of all he had experienced?

_____

_____

_____

_____

4. As you reflect on what you learned this week in Chapter 11, what is your biggest takeaway?

_____

_____

_____

_____

—TELL THE STORY—

As we go through *The Story* together, we want to learn how to tell the story. This week we will begin our focus on Movement 3. Read Movement 3 aloud together to begin to commit it to memory.

✝ Movement 3: The Story of Jesus (Matthew – John)

Jesus left the Upper Story to come down into our Lower Story to be with us and to provide the way for us to be made right with God. Through faith in Christ's work on the cross, we can now overturn Adam's choice and have a personal relationship with God.

PRAY TOGETHER

One of the most important things we can do together in community is to pray for each other and those around us. Review your prayer requests from last week, and look for ways God has answered the prayers of your group. Then use the space below to record prayer requests and praises for this week. Also, make sure to pray by name for people God might add to your group — especially your neighbors.

Name   *Request/Praise*

_____   _____

_____   _____

_____   _____

_____   _____

NEXT WEEK

Next week we'll look at the story of David's struggles and how one careless sin led to adultery, deceit, and murder.

Know the Story Answer Key — c / a / b / d

Video Notes Answer Key — cow / runt / forsaken / heart / shepherded / Messiah

The Trials of a King

"Create in me a pure heart, O God, and renew
a steadfast spirit in me. Do not cast me from
your presence or take your Holy Spirit from
me. Restore to me the joy of your salvation
and grant me a willing spirit, to sustain me."

PSALM 51:10 – 12

David's reign	David and Bathsheba	Solomon's reign	Temple building
BC 1010–970		970–930	966–959

Personal Time

Last week we looked at the story of David's rise to power. Perhaps you were encouraged by the way the Lord protected him and blessed his faithful youth.

This week before your Group Time and your weekend worship experience, spend time using the Personal Time section of your study guide to allow the story of David's trials and forgiveness to take root in your heart.

---KNOW THE STORY---

Before reading Chapter 12 of *The Story*, answer the questions below to test your knowledge of this week's Scripture. Enter your answers in the column marked "1st Time."

Question	1st Time	2nd Time
1		
2		
3		
4		

1. After Nathan confronted David, what was David's confession?
    a. I have sinned against Bathsheba.
    b. I have sinned against my other wives.
    c. I have sinned against the Lord.
    d. I have sinned against Uriah.

2. What was the result of Nathan confronting David over his sin with Bathsheba?
    a. David pleaded for the life of the child.
    b. David put on sackcloth and spent the nights lying on the ground.
    c. The child died.
    d. All of the above.

3. What ultimately happened to David's son Absalom?
    a. He became David's replacement as the next king over Israel.
    b. David's soldiers killed him while he hung in a tree by his hair.
    c. He died in battle with the Philistines.
    d. He was passed over as king and became bitter toward his brother.

4. What did David do to build the temple for the Lord?
    a. David provided all of the supplies necessary but did not build it.
    b. David hired skilled craftsmen from all over the region to help build it.
    c. David used slaves from some of the conquered countries to build it.
    d. David made the Israelites give a tithe of their time to build it.

Now read Chapter 12 of *The Story*. After reading, go back through to check your answers. Put your new answers in the column marked "2nd Time." (The answer key is found at the end of the session.)

UNDERSTAND THE STORY

As you read Chapter 12 of *The Story* during the week, allow the story of David's trials help you see the dangers of temptation and the power of forgiveness.

1. In the story of David and Bathsheba, what were the various ways the Lord tried to warn David away from his path of sin and toward repentance?

2. Look at all of the things David does in his repentance. What things do you learn from his example that you need to put into practice in your life?

3. Do you think things turned out for Absalom in a just way? Why or why not?

4. As you look at the story surrounding the preparation for the temple, how does this extravagance toward God affect your view of generosity?

5. After reading Chapter 12, what is one question you wish you could ask God about what you have read?

_____

_____

_____

_____

LIVE THE STORY

TAKE ACTION

We don't want to simply be hearers of the Word but also doers of the Word. Take some time to reflect on what you have read and studied this week.

1. Did you have a new discovery from your reading and study this week? If so, what was it?

_____

_____

_____

_____

2. Is there something you need to do based on what you learned?

_____

_____

_____

_____

3. Who can you tell about what you learned? Make a plan right now to share with that person.

_____

_____

_____

_____

—————————————TELL THE STORY—————————————

As we go through *The Story* together, we want to learn how to tell the story. This week we will continue to focus on Movement 3. Read Movement 3 below several times as you continue to commit it to memory.

✚ Movement 3: The Story of Jesus (Matthew–John)

Jesus left the _____ Story to come down into our Lower Story to be with us and to provide the way for us to be made right with God. Through faith in Christ's work on the cross, we can now overturn Adam's choice and have a personal _____ with God.

CONVERSATION

One day around a meal or your dinner table, have an intentional conversation about this week's topic. During the meal, read Psalm 51:10–12 found at the beginning of this session. Use the following question for discussion:

> How do we seek forgiveness in our relationship with God and in our relationships with others?

PRAY TOGETHER

Focusing the last thoughts of our day on God can help us rest — truly rest — in him. Each night read and reflect on Psalm 51:10–12, either on your own or with others if there are others living in your home. Pray and ask God to help you fully embrace David's story of seeking forgiveness. As you do this each night before bed, let the power of the verses impact both heart and mind.

● ● ●

Group Time

Welcome

Welcome to Session 12 of *The Story*. If there are any new members in your group, take time for introductions. You might open with a brief prayer asking God to help you understand and embrace the story of David.

KNOW THE STORY

Use one or both of these questions before you watch the video together.

1. How did you do on the quiz in the Know the Story section before you read the chapter?

_____

_____

_____

2. What was your most interesting insight or question from your Personal Time this week?

_____

_____

_____

UNDERSTAND THE STORY

As you watch the video for Session 12 of The Story, *use the section below to record some of the main points. (The answer key is found at the end of the session.)*

- There is something inside us that compels us to do

  _____.

- Uriah's _____ exposes the contrast with David's integrity.

- Nathan _____ the right to be heard.

- Sometimes when we do wrong, we set _____ consequences in motion.

- God includes the _____ likely candidates in his Upper Story.

————————————**LIVE THE STORY**————————————

TAKE ACTION

1. What part of Randy's teaching encouraged or challenged you the most? Why?

    ....

    ....

    ....

2. Did anything from your Personal Time jump out, calling you to action? Did anyone have an "aha" moment?

    ....

    ....

    ....

CONVERSATION

Have someone in your group read aloud the Case Study below and then discuss the questions that follow.

Sal and James were friends and neighbors whose children played together almost every day. Earlier in the day, a window had been broken at Sal's house while the boys were playing outside. When confronted by the two dads, both boys denied responsibility. In private, the two friends started talking about what to do. Sal said, "If my son had broken the window, he would admit it. We talk to him all the time about the importance of just admitting when you do something wrong. He has to be covering for your son." James could feel his temper starting to rise. James taught his son the same values. This conversation was about to ratchet up to a new level.

1. What do you think James should say and do if he wants to have a heart like David?

2. Based on what you read and learned this week, what counsel would you give to both Sal and James? What do you think they should say to the boys?

——————————TELL THE STORY——————————

As we go through The Story together, we want to learn how to tell the story. This week we will continue our focus on Movement 3. Read Movement 3 aloud together to continue to commit it to memory.

✝ Movement 3: The Story of Jesus (Matthew–John)

Jesus left the _____ Story to come down into our Lower Story to be with us and to provide the way for us to be made right with God. Through faith in Christ's work on the cross, we can now overturn Adam's choice and have a personal _____ with God.

——————————PRAY TOGETHER——————————

One of the most important things we can do together in community is to pray for each other and those around us. Review your prayer requests from last week, and look for ways God has answered the prayers of your group. Then use the space below to record prayer requests and praises for this week. Also, make sure to pray by name for people God might add to your group — especially your neighbors.

Name   Request/Praise

_____   _____

_____   _____

_____   _____

_____   _____

——————————NEXT WEEK——————————

Next week we'll look at the story of how God blessed Solomon with the most amazing kingdom in Israel's history.

Know the Story Answer Key — c / d / b / a

Video Notes Answer Key — wrong / integrity / earned / unstoppable / least

The King Who Had It All

> "Pride goes before destruction, a
> haughty spirit before a fall."

PROVERBS 16:18

	David dies	Solomon's reign	Solomon displays great wisdom	Temple building
BC	970	970–930		966–959

Personal Time

Last week we looked at the story of David's sin, repentance, and trials. Perhaps you were challenged to have more of a heart like David.

This week before your Group Time and your weekend worship experience, spend time using the Personal Time section of your study guide to allow the story of Solomon to take root in your heart.

---------------------**KNOW THE STORY**---------------------

Before reading Chapter 13 of *The Story*, answer the questions below to test
your knowledge of this week's Scripture. Enter your answers in the column
marked "1st Time."

Question	1st Time	2nd Time
1		
2		
3		
4		

1. Solomon asked the Lord for one thing. What did the Lord give him?
    a. Wisdom.
    b. Honor.
    c. Wealth.
    d. All of the above.

2. Which one of the proverbs below is not found in Solomon's writings?
    a. Honor the Lord with your wealth.
    b. The Lord helps those who help themselves
    c. Every fool is quick to quarrel.
    d. Haughty eyes and a proud heart produce sin.

3. When the temple was completed, what was the one thing the Lord wanted?
    a. The Lord wanted the humble hearts of the people.
    b. The Lord wanted a giant worship service.
    c. The Lord wanted large sacrifices of animals.
    d. The Lord wanted a huge offering to be taken for the temple.

4. What was the cause of Solomon's eventual downfall?
    a. He failed to build the temple for the Lord.
    b. The armies of the Queen of Sheba attacked him.
    c. He loved many foreign women and followed their gods.
    d. Hiram of Tyre refused to give Solomon necessary supplies for the temple.

Now read Chapter 13 of *The Story*. After reading, go back through to check
your answers. Put your new answers in the column marked "2nd Time." (The
answer key is found at the end of the session.)

————————————**UNDERSTAND THE STORY**————————————

As you read Chapter 13 of *The Story* during the week, allow the story of Solomon to help you see the abundant blessings God gave to him.

1. What do you see in the heart of God by the way he responds to Solomon's request for wisdom?

    _____

    _____

    _____

    _____

    _____

2. As you read through the proverbs on pages 179 – 183, write down two or three that have special significance to you. Why did you choose those?

    _____

    _____

    _____

    _____

    _____

3. What, to you, is the most important event in the building and dedication of the temple as you read through the various descriptions of what occurred?

    _____

    _____

    _____

    _____

    _____

4. What do you take as your personal warning in the downfall of Solomon?

    _____

    _____

    _____

    _____

5.   After reading Chapter 13, what is one question you wish you could ask
     God about what you have read?

_____

_____

_____

_____

—————————————————LIVE THE STORY———————————————

TAKE ACTION

We don't want to simply be hearers of the Word but also doers of the Word.
Take some time to reflect on what you have read and studied this week.

1.   Did you have a new discovery from your reading and study this week? If
     so, what was it?

_____

_____

_____

_____

2.   Is there something you need to do based on what you learned?

_____

_____

_____

_____

3.   Who can you tell about what you learned? Make a plan right now to
     share with that person.

_____

_____

_____

_____

TELL THE STORY

As we go through *The Story* together, we want to learn how to tell the story. This week we will continue to focus on Movement 3. Read Movement 3 below several times as you continue to commit it to memory.

✝ Movement 3: The Story of Jesus (Matthew – John)

Jesus left the _____ Story to come down into our Lower Story to be with us and to provide the way for us to be made _____ with God. Through faith in Christ's work on the _____, we can now overturn Adam's choice and have a personal _____ with God.

CONVERSATION

One day around a meal or your dinner table, have an intentional conversation about this week's topic. During the meal, read Proverbs 16:18 found at the beginning of this session. Use the following question for discussion:

> What are different ways we can avoid pride in our lives?

PRAY TOGETHER

Focusing the last thoughts of our day on God can help us rest — truly rest — in him. Each night read and reflect on Proverbs 16:18, either on your own or with others if there are others living in your home. Pray and ask God to help you fully embrace the warnings in the story of Solomon. As you do this each night before bed, let the power of the verse impact both heart and mind.

● ● ●

Group Time

Welcome

Welcome to Session 13 of *The Story*. If there are new members in your group, take time for introductions. You might open with a brief prayer asking God to help you understand and embrace the story of Solomon.

KNOW THE STORY

Use one or both of these questions before you watch the video together.

1. How did you do on the quiz in the Know the Story section before you read the chapter?

2. What was your most interesting insight or question from your Personal Time this week?

UNDERSTAND THE STORY

As you watch the video for Session 13 of The Story, *use the section below to record some of the main points. (The answer key is found at the end of the session.)*

- Solomon asked for _____ to carry out his duties.

- Solomon gave the baby to the _____ woman.

- Solomon started strong, but he finished _____.

- Solomon did _____ in the eyes of the Lord.

- We jump into a pot of _____ water, and the devil turns up the heat.

- _____ God and keep his commandments.

————————————LIVE THE STORY————————————

TAKE ACTION

1. What part of Randy's teaching encouraged or challenged you the most? Why?

2. Did anything from your Personal Time jump out, calling you to action? Did anyone have an "aha" moment?

CONVERSATION

Use one or two of the questions below (depending on time) to have a conversation in community.

1. Solomon's wisdom is still of great value to us today. What piece of wisdom from Solomon would you like to keep as a constant reminder this week?

2. Building the temple was one of the most important events in the history of Israel. Why do you think the temple was such an important part of Israel's culture?

3. Solomon went from the most powerful king in the world to his own downfall. What is the biggest warning for you in the story of the king who had it all?

4. As you reflect on what you learned this week in Chapter 13, what is your biggest takeaway?

_____

_____

_____

———————————TELL THE STORY———————————

As we go through *The Story* together, we want to learn how to tell the story. This week we will continue our focus on Movement 3. Read Movement 3 aloud together to continue to commit it to memory.

✝ Movement 3: The Story of Jesus (Matthew–John)

Jesus left the _____ Story to come down into our Lower Story to be with us and to provide the way for us to be made _____ with God. Through faith in Christ's work on the _____, we can now overturn Adam's choice and have a personal _____ with God.

———————————PRAY TOGETHER———————————

One of the most important things we can do together in community is to pray for each other and those around us. Review your prayer requests from last week, and look for ways God has answered the prayers of your group. Then use the space below to record prayer requests and praises for this week. Also, make sure to pray by name for people God might add to your group — especially your neighbors.

Name   *Request/Praise*

_____   _____

_____   _____

_____   _____

_____   _____

———————————NEXT WEEK———————————

Next week we'll look at how, after Solomon's death, the kingdom of Israel was torn in two by a young king who listened to poor counsel.

Know the Story Answer Key — d / b / a / c

Video Notes Answer Key — wisdom / second / poorly / evil / lukewarm / Fear

A Kingdom Torn in Two

"Your father put a heavy yoke on us, but now lighten the harsh labor and the heavy yoke he put on us, and we will serve you."

1 KINGS 12:4

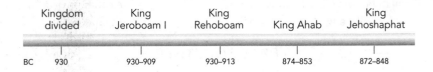

	Kingdom divided	King Jeroboam I	King Rehoboam	King Ahab	King Jehoshaphat
BC	930	930–909	930–913	874–853	872–848

Personal Time

Last week we looked at the story of Solomon. Perhaps you were challenged to make sure to not let the lukewarm temptations of life pull you away from God's best.

This week before your Group Time and your weekend worship experience, spend time using the Personal Time section of your study guide to allow the story of the divided kingdom to take root in your heart.

KNOW THE STORY

Before reading Chapter 14 of *The Story*, answer the questions below to test your knowledge of this week's Scripture. Enter your answers in the column marked "1st Time."

Question	1st Time	2nd Time
1		
2		
3		
4		

1. What group did Rehoboam make the mistake of listening to for counsel?
   a. The elders who had served his father Solomon.
   b. His wife who had given him good counsel in the past.
   c. The young men who had grown up with him.
   d. A group of kings from the surrounding nations.

2. What was the reason for Jeroboam's eventual downfall?
   a. He made other gods for himself.
   b. He attacked Rehoboam to try to take over the southern kingdom.
   c. He died of leprosy.
   d. He was murdered by one of his servants.

3. Which of the following was considered one of the good kings?
   a. Jeroboam
   b. Asa
   c. Abijah
   d. Ahab

4. Which is the chronological sequence of the kings of Judah?
   a. Solomon, Jeroboam, Baasha, Zimri
   b. Solomon, Rehoboam, Jeroboam, Asa
   c. Solomon, Rehoboam, Asa, Zimri
   d. Solomon, Rehoboam, Abijah, Asa

Now read Chapter 14 of *The Story*. After reading, revisit the questions to check your answers. Put your new answers in the column marked "2nd Time." (The answer key is found at the end of the session.)

————————UNDERSTAND THE STORY————————

As you read Chapter 14 of *The Story* during the week, allow the story of the divided kingdom to help you see the way the Lord continued to reach out to his people.

1. From where do you seek counsel when you have decisions to make? How do you make decisions when you seek counsel?

2. What are the things Jeroboam did to reject the Lord leading him as king? What do we learn about the Lord in those interactions with Jeroboam?

3. In the description of Asa on page 200, what important steps did he take to fully follow the Lord?

4. How would you explain a good king having a son who turned against the Lord completely? Why is this often difficult for us to understand?

5. After reading Chapter 14, what is one question you wish you could ask God about what you have read?

    _____

    _____

    _____

    _____

———————————**LIVE THE STORY**———————————

TAKE ACTION

We don't want to simply be hearers of the Word but also doers of the Word. Take some time to reflect on what you have read and studied this week.

1. Did you have a new discovery from your reading and study this week? If so, what was it?

    _____

    _____

    _____

    _____

2. Is there something you need to do based on what you learned?

    _____

    _____

    _____

    _____

3. Who can you tell about what you learned? Make a plan right now to share with that person.

    _____

    _____

    _____

    _____

TELL THE STORY

As we go through *The Story* together, we want to learn how to tell the story. This week we will continue to focus on Movement 3. Read Movement 3 several times as you continue to commit it to memory.

✚ Movement 3: The Story of Jesus (Matthew–John)

Jesus left the _____ Story to come down into our _____ Story to be with us and to provide the way for us to be made _____ with God. Through faith in Christ's work on the _____, we can now overturn _____ choice and have a personal _____ with God.

CONVERSATION

One day around a meal or your dinner table, have an intentional conversation about this week's topic. During the meal, read 1 Kings 12:4 found at the beginning of this session. Use the following question for discussion:

> What are pieces of advice you have received that you put into practice?

PRAY TOGETHER

Focusing the last thoughts of our day on God can help us rest — truly rest — in him. Each night read and reflect on 1 Kings 12:4, either on your own or with others if there are others living in your home. Pray and ask God to help you fully embrace the warnings in the lives of the various kings. As you do this each night before bed, let the power of the verse impact both heart and mind.

● ● ●

Group Time

Welcome

Welcome to Session 14 of *The Story*. If there are any new members in your group, take time for introductions. You might open with a brief prayer asking God to help you understand and embrace the story of the divided kingdom.

KNOW THE STORY

Use one or both of these questions before you watch the video together.

1. How did you do on the quiz in the Know the Story section before you read the chapter?

   _____

   _____

   _____

2. What was your most interesting insight or question from your Personal Time this week?

   _____

   _____

   _____

UNDERSTAND THE STORY

As you watch the video for Session 14 of The Story, *use the section below to record some of the main points. (The answer key is found at the end of the session.)*

- The Lower Story is how _____ see the story unfold.
- The Upper Story is how _____ sees the story unfold.
- King Rehoboam goes with the advice of the _____ men.
- When we are divided within, we will eventually _____.
- Israel was completely _____ the Upper Story of God.
- We need to align our _____ to his Upper Story plan.

LIVE THE STORY

TAKE ACTION

1. What part of Randy's teaching encouraged or challenged you the most? Why?

2. Did anything from your Personal Time jump out, calling you to action? Did anyone have an "aha" moment?

CONVERSATION

Have someone in your group read aloud the Case Study below and then discuss the questions that follow.

For years, Lisa and Jenny had been meeting once a month for lunch. They had encouraged each other as their children had grown, and now they shared updates on adult children and new grandchildren. Jenny had good stories about her two adult daughters, but the tears started to flow as she described her son. His marriage was about to end, and his drinking was out of control. Jenny worried about his two young children growing up without their dad present. Both adult girls were active in their churches, but her son had rejected the church and his faith years ago. "How could three children who were raised in the same Christian home end up so different? What did I do wrong?"

1. What do you think Lisa should say to Jenny to encourage her as she faces the challenges in her family?

2. Based on what you read and learned this week, how should the body of Christ respond to the seemingly inevitable stories of prodigals?

————————————TELL THE STORY————————————

As we go through *The Story* together, we want to learn how to tell the story. This week we will continue our focus on Movement 3. Read Movement 3 aloud together to continue to commit it to memory.

✝ Movement 3: The Story of Jesus (Matthew–John)

Jesus left the _____ Story to come down into our _____ Story to be with us and to provide the way for us to be made _____ with God. Through faith in Christ's work on the _____, we can now overturn _____ choice and have a personal _____ with God.

————————————PRAY TOGETHER————————————

One of the most important things we can do together in community is to pray for each other and those around us. Review your prayer requests from last week, and look for ways God has answered the prayers of your group. Then use the space below to record prayer requests and praises for this week. Also, make sure to pray by name for people God might add to your group — especially your neighbors.

Name   *Request/Praise*

_____   _____

_____   _____

_____   _____

_____   _____

————————————NEXT WEEK————————————

Next week we'll look at the story of God's messengers and how the Lord used these prophets to speak powerfully into the lives of the people of Israel.

Know the Story Answer Key — c / a / b / d

Video Notes Answer Key — we / God / younger / crumble / distorting / lives

God's Messengers

"I will heal their waywardness and
love them freely, for my anger has
turned away from them."

HOSEA 14:4

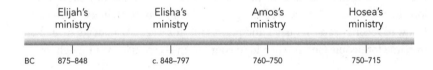

Elijah's ministry	Elisha's ministry	Amos's ministry	Hosea's ministry
BC 875–848	c. 848–797	760–750	750–715

Personal Time

Last week we looked at the story of the divided kingdom. Perhaps you were challenged in seeing how the kingdom fell apart when kings did not follow the Lord with all their hearts.

This week before your Group Time and your weekend worship experience, spend time using the Personal Time section of your study guide to allow the stories of the prophets of God to take root in your heart.

KNOW THE STORY

Before reading Chapter 15 of *The Story*, answer the questions below to test your knowledge of this week's Scripture. Enter your answers in the column marked "1st Time."

Question	1st Time	2nd Time
1		
2		
3		
4		

1. What happened after Elijah defeated the prophets of Baal?
   a. There was a great celebration and feast with the people of Israel.
   b. The people attacked Elijah in anger for destroying their gods.
   c. There was a tremendous rain that came down after a long time of drought.
   d. The people went out to destroy all of the temples of Baal.

2. How did the Lord make his appearance to Elijah in the wilderness?
   a. The Lord came in a great and powerful wind.
   b. The Lord came in a gentle whisper.
   c. The Lord came in a rumbling earthquake.
   d. The Lord came in a blazing fire.

3. How did Elijah die?
   a. Jezebel killed him after he destroyed the prophets of Baal.
   b. He died at a good old age full of life, wisdom, and blessing.
   c. Elisha replaced him as Israel's prophet, so Elijah killed himself.
   d. He was taken up to heaven in a whirlwind on a chariot of fire.

4. In the battle against Aram, how did the Lord use Elisha to defeat them?
   a. They were struck with blindness and led into their enemy's hands.
   b. Fear overtook the camp, and the men began to fight each other.
   c. The Lord made the sun stand still in the sky as they fought.
   d. Whenever Elisha's hands were raised, the Israelites were victorious.

Now read Chapter 15 of *The Story*. After reading, revisit the questions to check your answers. Put your new answers in the column marked "2nd Time." (The answer key is found at the end of the session.)

---UNDERSTAND THE STORY---

As you read Chapter 15 of *The Story* during the week, allow the story of the prophets to help you see how the Lord continued to speak to his people even when they were disobedient to him.

1. Which part of the story of Elijah and the prophets of Baal do you think had the greatest impact on the Israelites? Why?

    _____

    _____

    _____

    _____

    _____

2. How would you describe what happened to Elijah when he fled into the wilderness after the encounter with the prophets of Baal?

    _____

    _____

    _____

    _____

3. As you read the descriptions of Elisha on pages 209 – 213, list all the ways the Lord used him to minister to the people of Israel.

    _____

    _____

    _____

    _____

4. Read the words of Amos and Hosea on pages 213 – 217. What is the purpose in the words Amos shares with the Israelites? What is the purpose of Hosea's words?

    _____

    _____

    _____

    _____

5. After reading Chapter 15, what is one question you wish you could ask God about what you have read?

_____

_____

_____

_____

LIVE THE STORY

TAKE ACTION

We don't want to simply be hearers of the Word but also doers of the Word. Take some time to reflect on what you have read and studied this week.

1. Did you have a new discovery from your reading and study this week? If so, what was it?

_____

_____

_____

_____

2. Is there something you need to do based on what you learned?

_____

_____

_____

_____

3. Who can you tell about what you learned? Make a plan right now to share with that person.

_____

_____

_____

_____

TELL THE STORY

This is our last week to focus on Movement 3. Read Movement 3 below several times, filling in the blanks until you have it committed to memory. Then see if you can say all of Movement 3 without looking.

✝ Movement 3: The Story of Jesus (Matthew–John)

Jesus left the _____ Story to come down into our _____ Story to be with us and to provide the _____ for us to be made _____ with God. Through _____ in Christ's work on the _____, we can now overturn _____ choice and have a personal _____ with God.

CONVERSATION

One day around a meal or your dinner table, have an intentional conversation about this week's topic. During the meal, read Hosea 14:4 found at the beginning of this session. Use the following question for discussion:

> What are different ways the Lord shows us his love and grace each day when we don't deserve it?

PRAY TOGETHER

Focusing the last thoughts of our day on God can help us rest — truly rest — in him. Each night read and reflect on Hosea 14:4, either on your own or with others if there are others living in your home. Pray and ask God to help you fully embrace the stories of his prophets. As you do this each night before bed, let the power of the verse impact both heart and mind.

● ● ●

Group Time

Welcome

Welcome to Session 15 of *The Story*. If there are any new members in your group, take time for introductions. You might open with a brief prayer asking God to help you understand and embrace the various stories of the prophets.

KNOW THE STORY

Use one or both of these questions before you watch the video together.

1. How did you do on the quiz in the Know the Story section before you read the chapter?

   _____

   _____

   _____

2. What was your most interesting insight or question from your Personal Time this week?

   _____

   _____

   _____

UNDERSTAND THE STORY

As you watch the video for Session 15 of The Story, *use the section below to record some of the main points. (The answer key is found at the end of the session.)*

- The secret of their success is their _____.
- God raised up prophets or _____.
- God asked Hosea to marry a _____.
- "_____, Israel, to the LORD your God."
- Maybe he's calling just to say he _____ you.

LIVE THE STORY

TAKE ACTION

1. What part of Randy's teaching encouraged or challenged you the most? Why?

2. Did anything from your Personal Time jump out, calling you to action? Did anyone have an "aha" moment?

CONVERSATION

Use one or two of the questions below (depending on time) to have a conversation in community.

1. Elijah and Elisha experienced incredible anointing by God. How do you see the lives of the Old Testament prophets aligning with the role of Christians today?

2. The prophets were often used to warn Israel of her poor choices in the Lower Story. Why did the Israelites so infrequently respond with repentance?

3. What is the role of the various miracles the Lord performed through the different prophets? Choose one miracle, and describe how the Lord used it.

4. As you reflect on what you learned this week in Chapter 15, what is your biggest takeaway?

_____

_____

_____

————————TELL THE STORY————————

As we go through *The Story* together, we want to learn how to tell the story. This is our last week to focus on Movement 3. Read Movement 3 aloud together, filling in the blanks as you commit it to memory. Then see if you can all say it together as a group.

✝ Movement 3: The Story of Jesus (Matthew–John)

Jesus left the _____ Story to come down into our _____ Story to be with us and to provide the _____ for us to be made _____ with God. Through _____ in Christ's work on the _____, we can now overturn _____ choice and have a personal _____ with God.

————————PRAY TOGETHER————————

One of the most important things we can do together in community is to pray for each other and those around us. Review your prayer requests from last week, and look for ways God has answered the prayers of your group. Then use the space below to record prayer requests and praises for this week. Also, make sure to pray by name for people God might add to your group — especially your neighbors.

Name   Request/Praise

_____   _____

_____   _____

_____   _____

_____   _____

————————NEXT WEEK————————

Next week we'll look at the story of the downfall of Israel and what happens as they are sent off to exile.

Know the Story Answer Key — c / b / d / a

Video Notes Answer Key — God / messengers / prostitute / Return / loves

The Beginning of the End (of the Kingdom of Israel)

> "Come, all you who are thirsty, come
> to the waters; and you who have no
> money, come, buy and eat!"

ISAIAH 55:1

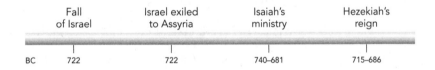

Fall of Israel	Israel exiled to Assyria	Isaiah's ministry	Hezekiah's reign
BC 722	722	740–681	715–686

Personal Time

Last week we looked at the story of God's messengers challenging the people of Israel. Perhaps you were encouraged to see how the Lord continued to pursue his people even when they were far from him.

This week before your Group Time and your weekend worship experience, spend time using the Personal Time section of your study guide to allow the stories of the fall of Israel and the prophetic words of Isaiah to take root in your heart.

—KNOW THE STORY—

Before reading Chapter 16 of *The Story*, answer the questions below to test your knowledge of this week's Scripture. Enter your answers in the column marked "1st Time."

Question	1st Time	2nd Time
1		
2		
3		
4		

1. How did Hezekiah respond when the Assyrians threatened to attack him?
   a. He assembled all the fighting men of Israel over the age of twenty.
   b. He went up to the temple of the Lord to pray.
   c. He sent word to the king of Cush to come to their aid.
   d. He made a peace treaty with King Sennacherib to spare his people.

2. What was Isaiah's response when he had a vision of the Lord seated on a throne?
   a. He said, "Great is the Lord and worthy to be praised!"
   b. He said nothing, and he got on his face in worship before the Lord.
   c. He said, "Woe to me! For I am a man of unclean lips!"
   d. He tore his clothes and put on sackcloth and ashes.

3. What were the prophetic words Isaiah spoke to Israel?
   a. The Lord will have compassion on you and settle you in your own land.
   b. Destruction is around the corner, and you will be sent in exile to Egypt.
   c. These are days of freedom and prosperity, but trouble is on the horizon.
   d. All of the above.

4. What are the words Isaiah speaks about a coming Messiah?
   a. He was led like a lamb to the slaughter.
   b. He had no beauty or majesty to attract us to him.
   c. The Lord has laid on him the iniquity of us all.
   d. All of the above.

Now read Chapter 16 of *The Story*. After reading, revisit the questions to check your answers. Put your new answers in the column marked "2nd Time." (The answer key is found at the end of the session.)

UNDERSTAND THE STORY

As you read Chapter 16 of *The Story* during the week, allow the story of the fall of Israel and the words of Isaiah to help you see the Lord's ultimate protection of Israel.

1. What do you see in the taunts of the leaders of Assyria that are similar to statements you hear or read against Christians today?

2. What traits do you see in Hezekiah that you would like to practice in your own life?

3. Briefly describe the Lower Story circumstances of the people of Israel. Now, what is the Upper Story you see prophesied for them?

4. As you read the description of the Messiah, which verse or description impacts you in the biggest way, and why?

5. After reading Chapter 16, what is one question you wish you could ask God about what you have read?

LIVE THE STORY

TAKE ACTION

We don't want to simply be hearers of the Word but also doers of the Word. Take some time to reflect on what you have read and studied this week.

1. Did you have a new discovery from your reading and study this week? If so, what was it?

2. Is there something you need to do based on what you learned?

3. Who can you tell about what you learned? Make a plan right now to share with that person.

---------------TELL THE STORY---------------

As we go through *The Story* together, we want to learn how to tell the story. This week we will begin to focus on Movement 4. Read Movement 4 below several times as you begin to commit it to memory.

 ## Movement 4: The Story of the Church (Acts–Jude)

Everyone who comes into a relationship with God through faith in Christ belongs to the new community God is building called the church. The church is commissioned to be the presence of Christ in the Lower Story—telling his story by the way we live and the words we speak. Every story of the church points people to the second coming of Christ, when he will return to restore God's original vision.

CONVERSATION

One day around a meal or your dinner table, have an intentional conversation about this week's topic. During the meal, read Isaiah 55:1 found at the beginning of this session. Use the following question for discussion:

> What does the Lord offer us when we come to him with open hands and hearts?

PRAY TOGETHER

Focusing the last thoughts of our day on God can help us rest—truly rest—in him. Each night read and reflect on Isaiah 55:1, either on your own or with others if there are others living in your home. Pray and ask God to help you fully embrace the promises in this week's story. As you do this each night before bed, let the power of the verse impact both heart and mind.

● ● ●

Group Time

Welcome

Welcome to Session 16 of *The Story*. If there are any new members in your group, take time for introductions. You might open with a brief prayer asking God to help you understand and embrace the story of God's promises in the midst of Israel's downfall.

KNOW THE STORY

Use one or both of these questions before you watch the video together.

1. How did you do on the quiz in the Know the Story section before you read the chapter?

   _____

   _____

   _____

2. What was your most interesting insight or question from your Personal Time this week?

   _____

   _____

   _____

UNDERSTAND THE STORY

As you watch the video for Session 16 of The Story, *use the section below to record some of the main points. (The answer key is found at the end of the session.)*

- God's prophets spoke to the northern kingdom for _____ years.

- Hezekiah did what was _____ in the eyes of the Lord.

- Isaiah told Hezekiah that God has got your _____.

- "Then you will know that I am the _____."

- No _____ but King Jesus.

---**LIVE THE STORY**---

TAKE ACTION

1. What part of Randy's teaching encouraged or challenged you the most? Why?

    _____

    _____

    _____

2. Did anything from your Personal Time jump out, calling you to action? Did anyone have an "aha" moment?

    _____

    _____

    _____

CONVERSATION

Have someone in your group read aloud the Case Study below and then discuss the questions that follow.

Simon and Jay got together every Thursday night with a few guys from their neighborhood to catch up and encourage each other. It was nothing fancy or formal—just a small group of guys hanging out in Simon's garage. This week Jay felt a need to unload. Stress at work had hit a new high when his department lost two people with no plans to refill the positions. While doing some yard work two nights ago, he had put his shovel through an underground cable cutting off service to their neighbor's TV. Yesterday, his teenage daughter totaled one of their cars. Thankfully, she was unhurt. Everything was piling up, and Jay felt he couldn't see light at the end of the tunnel—unless it was the light of an oncoming train.

1. As you consider your current circumstances, in what ways can you relate to Jay?

2. Based on what you read and learned this week, how could Simon share an Upper Story perspective with Jay without sounding trite or cliché?

---TELL THE STORY---

As we go through *The Story* together, we want to learn how to tell the story. This week we will begin our focus on Movement 4. Read Movement 4 aloud together to begin to commit it to memory.

Movement 4: The Story of the Church (Acts–Jude)

Everyone who comes into a relationship with God through faith in Christ belongs to the new community God is building called the church. The church is commissioned to be the presence of Christ in the Lower Story — telling his story by the way we live and the words we speak. Every story of the church points people to the second coming of Christ, when he will return to restore God's original vision.

---PRAY TOGETHER---

One of the most important things we can do together in community is to pray for each other and those around us. Review your prayer requests from last week, and look for ways God has answered the prayers of your group. Then use the space below to record prayer requests and praises for this week. Also, make sure to pray by name for people God might add to your group — especially your neighbors.

Name   *Request/Praise*

_____   _____

_____   _____

_____   _____

_____   _____

---NEXT WEEK---

Next week we'll look at the stories of the final kings of Judah leading to Jerusalem's eventual fall and exile into Babylon.

Know the Story Answer Key — b / c / a / d

Video Notes Answer Key — 208 / right / back / Lord / king

The Kingdoms' Fall

"The LORD is good to those whose hope is in him, to the one who seeks him; it is good to wait quietly for the salvation of the LORD."

LAMENTATIONS 3:25 – 26

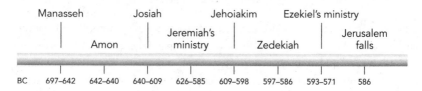

Manasseh		Josiah		Jehoiakim		Ezekiel's ministry	
	Amon		Jeremiah's ministry		Zedekiah		Jerusalem falls

BC	697–642	642–640	640–609	626–585	609–598	597–586	593–571	586

Personal Time

Last week we looked at the story of the fall of Israel along with Isaiah's prophetic words of a Messiah. Perhaps you were challenged to see the Upper Story of God in the midst of Lower Story turmoil.

This week before your Group Time and your weekend worship experience, spend time using the Personal Time section of your study guide to allow the story of the lower kingdom of Judah's exile into Babylon to take root in your heart.

KNOW THE STORY

Before reading Chapter 17 of *The Story*, answer the questions below to test your knowledge of this week's Scripture. Enter your answers in the column marked "1st Time."

Question	1st Time	2nd Time
1		
2		
3		
4		

1. Which of the following is a good description of Manasseh?
   a. Manasseh shed so much innocent blood that he filled Jerusalem.
   b. Manasseh sacrificed his own son in the fire, practiced divination, sought omens, and consulted mediums and spiritists.
   c. Manasseh humbled himself and knew that the Lord is God.
   d. All of the above.

2. Who is described as the "weeping prophet"?
   a. Ezekiel
   b. Jeremiah
   c. Josiah
   d. Manasseh

3. Why did Zedekiah ask for one more inquiry of the Lord?
   a. He was hoping for the Lord to perform wonders as in times past.
   b. He was trying to determine the timing of their attack.
   c. He wanted to know with certainty the plans the Lord had given him.
   d. This was Zedekiah's normal practice prior to entering a battle.

4. In one of Ezekiel's final prophecies, to what was he called to prophesy?
   a. A broken spear.
   b. A ruined temple.
   c. A valley of dry bones.
   d. An empty tomb.

Now read Chapter 17 of *The Story*. After reading, revisit the questions to check your answers. Put your new answers in the column marked "2nd Time." (The answer key is found at the end of the session.)

——————————UNDERSTAND THE STORY——————————

As you read Chapter 17 of *The Story* during the week, allow the story of the fall of Jerusalem to help you see how God does not abandon his people in the Upper Story.

1. What are the common traits and practices you see in the kings who did evil before the Lord? What are the common traits and practices in the kings who did good in God's sight?

2. What would it be like to have a vision or experience similar to Ezekiel's encounter with God described on page 235?

3. Read Jeremiah's prophecy on pages 238 – 240. What was the message he was trying to deliver to Jerusalem?

4. What are ways the reign of the last king, Zedekiah, served as the final straw for the people of Jerusalem? How did it end for them?

5. After reading Chapter 17, what is one question you wish you could ask God about what you have read?

_____

_____

_____

_____

_____

LIVE THE STORY

TAKE ACTION

We don't want to simply be hearers of the Word but also doers of the Word. Take some time to reflect on what you have read and studied this week.

1. Did you have a new discovery from your reading and study this week? If so, what was it?

_____

_____

_____

_____

_____

2. Is there something you need to do based on what you learned?

_____

_____

_____

_____

_____

3. Who can you tell about what you learned? Make a plan right now to share with that person.

_____

_____

_____

_____

_____

---------------------------TELL THE STORY---------------------------

As we go through *The Story* together, we want to learn how to tell the story. This week we will continue to focus on Movement 4. Read Movement 4 several times as you continue to commit it to memory.

∞ Movement 4: The Story of the Church (Acts – Jude)

Everyone who comes into a relationship with God through faith in Christ belongs to the new community God is building called the _____. The church is commissioned to be the presence of Christ in the Lower Story — telling his story by the way we live and the words we speak. Every story of the church points people to the _____ coming of Christ, when he will return to restore God's original vision.

CONVERSATION

One day around a meal or your dinner table, have an intentional conversation about this week's topic. During the meal, read Lamentations 3:25 – 26 found at the beginning of this session. Use the following question for discussion:

> What are ways we can put our hope in God, seek him, and wait quietly for him?

PRAY TOGETHER

Focusing the last thoughts of our day on God can help us rest — truly rest — in him. Each night read and reflect on Lamentations 3:25 – 26, either on your own or with others if there are others living in your home. Pray and ask God to help you fully embrace the story of Judah's exile into Babylon. As you do this each night before bed, let the power of the verses impact both heart and mind.

● ● ●

Group Time

Welcome

Welcome to Session 17 of *The Story*. If there are any new members in your group, take time for introductions. You might open with a brief prayer asking God to help you understand and embrace the story of Jerusalem's fall.

KNOW THE STORY

Use one or both of these questions before you watch the video together.

1. How did you do on the quiz in the Know the Story section before you read the chapter?

   _____

   _____

   _____

2. What was your most interesting insight or question from your Personal Time this week?

   _____

   _____

   _____

UNDERSTAND THE STORY

As you watch the video for Session 17 of The Story, *use the section below to record some of the main points. (The answer key is found at the end of the session.)*

- People would see how life in _____ works.

- The story tells us Manasseh did _____ evil.

- " ... when I am proved _____ through you before their eyes."

- He already has things in mind for you if you will _____ your life to the Upper Story of God.

- _____ is faithfulness to God, not results.

———————————LIVE THE STORY———————————

TAKE ACTION

1. What part of Randy's teaching encouraged or challenged you the most? Why?

———————————————————————————————————

———————————————————————————————————

2. Did anything from your Personal Time jump out, calling you to action? Did anyone have an "aha" moment?

———————————————————————————————————

———————————————————————————————————

CONVERSATION

Use one or two of the questions below (depending on time) to have a conversation in community.

1. Over the last few chapters, we have looked at good kings and bad kings. What are the common characteristics of the good kings? Which king was your favorite, and why?

———————————————————————————————————

———————————————————————————————————

———————————————————————————————————

2. What are the common characteristics of the bad kings? What are the warnings for us today in reading about those kings?

———————————————————————————————————

———————————————————————————————————

———————————————————————————————————

3. As you read about the fall of Jerusalem and Judah's exile, provide a two- or three-sentence summary for what happened to this nation.

———————————————————————————————————

———————————————————————————————————

———————————————————————————————————

4. As you reflect on what you learned this week in Chapter 17, what is your biggest takeaway?

———————————————————————————————————

———————————————————————————————————

———————————————————————————————————

---────**TELL THE STORY**────---

As we go through *The Story* together, we want to learn how to tell the story. This week we will continue our focus on Movement 4. Read Movement 4 aloud together to continue to commit it to memory.

✚ Movement 4: The Story of the Church (Acts–Jude)

Everyone who comes into a relationship with God through faith in Christ belongs to the new community God is building called the _____. The church is commissioned to be the presence of Christ in the Lower Story — telling his story by the way we live and the words we speak. Every story of the church points people to the _____ coming of Christ, when he will return to restore God's original vision.

---────**PRAY TOGETHER**────---

One of the most important things we can do together in community is to pray for each other and those around us. Review your prayer requests from last week, and look for ways God has answered the prayers of your group. Then use the space below to record prayer requests and praises for this week. Also, make sure to pray by name for people God might add to your group — especially your neighbors.

Name   *Request/Praise*

_____   _____

_____   _____

_____   _____

_____   _____

---────**NEXT WEEK**────---

Next week we'll look at the story of Daniel and how the Lord showed favor on his people even in the midst of their exile in Babylon.

Know the Story Answer Key — d / b / a / c

Video Notes Answer Key — community / much / holy / align / Success

Daniel in Exile

"For he is the living God and he endures
forever; his kingdom will not be destroyed,
his dominion will never end. He rescues
and he saves; he performs signs and
wonders in the heavens and on the earth."

DANIEL 6:26 – 27

Daniel exiled to Babylon	Daniel's ministry	Nebuchad-nezzar	Daniel and the lions' den	Babylon falls
BC 605	605–536	605–562	539	539

Personal Time

Last week we looked at the story of Jerusalem's fall and Judah's exile. Perhaps you were warned by what happened to them and their eventual downfall.

This week before your Group Time and your weekend worship experience, spend time using the Personal Time section of your study guide to allow the story of Daniel in exile to take root in your heart.

KNOW THE STORY

Before reading Chapter 18 of *The Story*, answer the questions below to test your knowledge of this week's Scripture. Enter your answers in the column marked "1st Time."

Question	1st Time	2nd Time
1		
2		
3		
4		

1. What special diet does Daniel request from the king's chief official?
   a. Royal meat and wine.
   b. Fruits and vegetables.
   c. Vegetables and water.
   d. Manna and quail.

2. What amazed the officials when Shadrach, Meshach, and Abednego came out of the fiery furnace?
   a. Not a hair on their heads was singed.
   b. Their robes were not scorched.
   c. They did not smell like smoke.
   d. All of the above.

3. Why was Daniel thrown into the den of lions?
   a. He refused to bow down to the golden idol of the king.
   b. He prayed to his God three times a day.
   c. Jealous enemies brought false accusations to the king.
   d. All of the above.

4. Which prophet predicted the return of the Israelites from captivity?
   a. Jeremiah
   b. Hezekiah
   c. Ezekiel
   d. Hosea

Now read Chapter 18 of *The Story*. After reading, revisit the questions to check your answers. Put your new answers in the column marked "2nd Time." (The answer key is found at the end of the session.)

─────── UNDERSTAND THE STORY ───────

As you read Chapter 18 of *The Story* during the week, allow the story of Daniel to help you see the Lord's faithfulness to his people even in the midst of exile in Babylon.

1. What significant decisions or actions did Daniel take leading up to his interpretation of the king's dream?

2. What can we learn from Shadrach, Meshach, and Abednego's response to the king's demand that the image be worshiped?

3. Daniel faced a difficult decision whether or not to defy the king's edict for worship. How can you foresee ways you might face a similar decision in our society today to make a radical stand for your faith?

4. As you read through the prophecies on pages 260 – 261, how do Jeremiah's words provide hope for you today?

5. After reading Chapter 18, what is one question you wish you could ask God about what you have read?

_____

_____

_____

_____

_____

LIVE THE STORY

TAKE ACTION

We don't want to simply be hearers of the Word but also doers of the Word. Take some time to reflect on what you have read and studied this week.

1. Did you have a new discovery from your reading and study this week? If so, what was it?

_____

_____

_____

_____

2. Is there something you need to do based on what you learned?

_____

_____

_____

_____

3. Who can you tell about what you learned? Make a plan right now to share with that person.

_____

_____

_____

_____

TELL THE STORY

As we go through *The Story* together, we want to learn how to tell the story. This week we will continue to focus on Movement 4. Read Movement 4 below several times as you continue to commit it to memory.

Movement 4: The Story of the Church (Acts–Jude)

Everyone who comes into a relationship with God through _____ in Christ belongs to the new community God is building called the _____. The church is commissioned to be the _____ of Christ in the Lower Story — telling his story by the way we live and the words we speak. Every story of the church points people to the _____ coming of Christ, when he will return to restore God's original vision.

CONVERSATION

One day around a meal or your dinner table, have an intentional conversation about this week's topic. During the meal, read Daniel 6:26 – 27 found at the beginning of this session. Use the following question for discussion:

> What does this verse mean to you when you read "he rescues and saves" and "performs signs and wonders"?

PRAY TOGETHER

Focusing the last thoughts of our day on God can help us rest — truly rest — in him. Each night read and reflect on Daniel 6:26 – 27, either on your own or with others if there are others living in your home. Pray and ask God to help you fully embrace the story of Daniel. As you do this each night before bed, let the power of the verses impact both heart and mind.

● ● ●

Group Time

Welcome

Welcome to Session 18 of *The Story*. If there are any new members in your group, take time for introductions. You might open with a brief prayer asking God to help you understand and embrace the story of Daniel.

KNOW THE STORY

Use one or both of these questions before you watch the video together.

1. How did you do on the quiz in the Know the Story section before you read the chapter?

2. What was your most interesting insight or question from your Personal Time this week?

UNDERSTAND THE STORY

As you watch the video for Session 18 of The Story, *use the section below to record some of the main points. (The answer key is found at the end of the session.)*

- Daniel _____ himself not to be defiled by the royal food and wine.

- Anyone who fails to bow down will be thrown in a fiery _____.

- Who said you have to do _____ to rise?

- In the Upper Story, the King of kings closes the mouths of lions for bowing _____ to him.

- "If he doesn't save me, I have no _____."

LIVE THE STORY

TAKE ACTION

1. What part of Randy's teaching encouraged or challenged you the most? Why?

_____

_____

_____

2. Did anything from your Personal Time jump out, calling you to action? Did anyone have an "aha" moment?

_____

_____

_____

CONVERSATION

Have someone in your group read aloud the Case Study below and then discuss the questions that follow.

Lynn had been with her company for eight years, and her annual reviews reflected a hardworking, conscientious team player. That's why her recent encounter with her supervisor, Christine, surprised her. Lynn had always had a few regular practices at work. Over her lunch hour, she would often take out her Bible to work on her weekly Bible study lesson. She also frequently ended conversations with coworkers with the phrase, "Have a blessed day." Occasionally, other employees would come to her sharing a request to pray for a life crisis, and Lynn always promised to pray for them. Now Christine has taken Lynn into her office to say, "A lot of your coworkers have been complaining about how you are so vocal about your faith in the workplace. Your prayers and comments and having your Bible out on your desk have made some of them describe this as a hostile work environment. I'm going to need you to stop doing these things."

1. Is Christine justified in her request to Lynn? Or do you think Christine has crossed the line of religious liberty?

2. Based on what you read and learned this week, how should Lynn respond?

―――――――――――――――TELL THE STORY―――――――――――――――

As we go through *The Story* together, we want to learn how to tell the story. This week we will continue our focus on Movement 4. Read Movement 4 aloud together to continue to commit it to memory.

◉ Movement 4: The Story of the Church (Acts–Jude)

Everyone who comes into a relationship with God through _____ in Christ belongs to the new community God is building called the _____. The church is commissioned to be the _____ of Christ in the Lower Story — telling his story by the way we live and the words we speak. Every story of the church points people to the _____ coming of Christ, when he will return to restore God's original vision.

―――――――――――――――PRAY TOGETHER―――――――――――――――

One of the most important things we can do together in community is to pray for each other and those around us. Review your prayer requests from last week, and look for ways God has answered the prayers of your group. Then use the space below to record prayer requests and praises for this week. Also, make sure to pray by name for people God might add to your group — especially your neighbors.

Name   *Request/Praise*

_____   _____

_____   _____

_____   _____

―――――――――――――――NEXT WEEK―――――――――――――――

Next week we'll look at the story of the incredible return home from exile for the people of Jerusalem along with the rebuilding of the temple.

Know the Story Answer Key — c / d / b / a

Video Notes Answer Key — resolved / furnace / wrong / only / regrets

The Return Home

"Give careful thought to your ways. You
have planted much, but harvested little.
You eat, but never have enough. You drink,
but never have your fill. You put on clothes,
but are not warm. You earn wages, only
to put them in a purse with holes in it."

HAGGAI 1:5 – 6

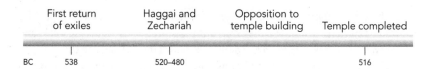

First return of exiles	Haggai and Zechariah	Opposition to temple building	Temple completed
BC 538	520–480		516

Personal Time

Last week we looked at the stories of Daniel and his friends. Perhaps you were challenged by their bold stand for faith in the midst of a religiously hostile society.

This week before your Group Time and your weekend worship experience, spend time using the Personal Time section of your study guide to allow the story of the return from exile to take root in your heart.

──────────── KNOW THE STORY ────────────

Before reading Chapter 19 of *The Story*, answer the questions below to test your knowledge of this week's Scripture. Enter your answers in the column marked "1st Time."

Question	1st Time	2nd Time
1		
2		
3		
4		

1. Who made the proclamation to rebuild the temple?
   a. The king of the Israelites
   b. Cyrus king of Persia
   c. Daniel
   d. Zechariah

2. What prophet did God send to encourage the Israelites to continue building?
   a. Haggai
   b. Jonah
   c. Daniel
   d. Isaiah

3. What prophetic message did Zechariah share with the people?
   a. Israel will crush and drive out her enemies.
   b. You will be punished for the sins of your fathers in this land.
   c. A greater day for Jerusalem is coming in the future.
   d. All of the above

4. Who issued the second proclamation helping to pay for all the building expenses?
   a. Cyrus
   b. Haggai
   c. Zechariah
   d. Darius

Now read Chapter 19 of *The Story*. After reading, revisit the questions to check your answers. Put your new answers in the column marked "2nd Time." (The answer key is found at the end of the session.)

—————————UNDERSTAND THE STORY—————————

As you read Chapter 19 of *The Story* during the week, allow the story of the return to the Promised Land in the Lower Story to help you clearly see God's continued plan for Israel in the Upper Story.

1. How did the Lord use Cyrus to further his plans? How does he sometimes use unlikely leaders (then and now) to further his plans for his people?

2. Why did Haggai need to speak a prophetic message of encouragement to the people?

3. What hope do you see in Zechariah's words to the people?

4. How did God use opposition to the building of the temple to do an even greater work of provision for his people?

5. After reading Chapter 19, what is one question you wish you could ask God about what you have read?

_____

_____

_____

_____

—————————————LIVE THE STORY—————————————

TAKE ACTION

We don't want to simply be hearers of the Word but also doers of the Word. Take some time to reflect on what you have read and studied this week.

1. Did you have a new discovery from your reading and study this week? If so, what was it?

_____

_____

_____

_____

2. Is there something you need to do based on what you learned?

_____

_____

_____

_____

3. Who can you tell about what you learned? Make a plan right now to share with that person.

_____

_____

_____

_____

TELL THE STORY

As we go through *The Story* together, we want to learn how to tell the story. This week we will continue to focus on Movement 4. Read Movement 4 several times as you continue to commit it to memory.

✸ Movement 4: The Story of the Church (Acts–Jude)

_____ who comes into a relationship with God through _____ in Christ belongs to the new community God is building called the _____. The church is commissioned to be the _____ of Christ in the Lower Story — telling his story by the way we live and the words we speak. Every story of the _____ points people to the _____ coming of Christ, when he will return to restore God's original vision.

CONVERSATION

One day around a meal or your dinner table, have an intentional conversation about this week's topic. During the meal, read Haggai 1:5 – 6 found at the beginning of this session. Use the following question for discussion:

> How can we sometimes work for more and more and end up with less and less?

PRAY TOGETHER

Focusing the last thoughts of our day on God can help us rest — truly rest — in him. Each night read and reflect on Haggai 1:5 – 6, either on your own or with others if there are others living in your home. Pray and ask God to help you fully embrace the story of the rebuilding of the temple. As you do this each night before bed, let the power of the verses impact both heart and mind.

● ● ●

Group Time

Welcome

Welcome to Session 19 of *The Story*. If there are any new members in your group, take time for introductions. You might open with a brief prayer asking God to help you understand and embrace the story of the rebuilding of the temple.

KNOW THE STORY

Use one or both of these questions before you watch the video together.

1. How did you do on the quiz in the Know the Story section before you read the chapter?

2. What was your most interesting insight or question from your Personal Time this week?

UNDERSTAND THE STORY

As you watch the video for Session 19 of The Story, *use the section below to record some of the main points. (The answer key is found at the end of the session.)*

- The Lord _____ the heart of Cyrus king of Persia.

- God's solution: Access through the _____ of blood.

- In the Lower Story, God's big thing became their _____ thing.

- There are seasons of God-ordained _____.

- "Go up into the mountains and bring down the timber and build the _____."

———————————**LIVE THE STORY**———————————

TAKE ACTION

1. What part of Randy's teaching encouraged or challenged you the most? Why?

2. Did anything from your Personal Time jump out, calling you to action? Did anyone have an "aha" moment?

CONVERSATION

Use one or two of the questions below (depending on time) to have a conversation in community.

1. How did the Lord use the kings of Persia to accomplish his plans? How has he done this in modern times?

2. How did the people face a subtle and gradual discouragement? Why do you think subtle and gradual discouragement is often more difficult to face and resist?

3. Summarize the specific messages the Lord delivers to his people through his two prophets.

4. As you reflect on what you learned this week in Chapter 19, what is your biggest takeaway?

_____

_____

_____

TELL THE STORY

As we go through *The Story* together, we want to learn how to tell the story. This week we will continue our focus on Movement 4. Read Movement 4 aloud together to continue to commit it to memory.

Movement 4: The Story of the Church (Acts–Jude)

_____ who comes into a relationship with God through _____ in Christ belongs to the new community God is building called the _____. The church is commissioned to be the _____ of Christ in the Lower Story — telling his story by the way we live and the words we speak. Every story of the _____ points people to the _____ coming of Christ, when he will return to restore God's original vision.

PRAY TOGETHER

One of the most important things we can do together in community is to pray for each other and those around us. Review your prayer requests from last week, and look for ways God has answered the prayers of your group. Then use the space below to record prayer requests and praises for this week. Also, make sure to pray by name for people God might add to your group — especially your neighbors.

Name   *Request/Praise*

_____   _____

_____   _____

_____   _____

NEXT WEEK

Next week we'll look at the story of Esther and how God orchestrated amazing details and timing to save his people from execution.

Know the Story Answer Key — b / a / c / d

Video Notes Answer Key — moved / shedding / small / struggles / house

The Queen of Beauty and Courage

"And who knows but that you have come to your royal position for such a time as this?"

ESTHER 4:14

	Xerxes	Esther becomes queen	Esther saves the Jews	Days of Purim
BC	486–465	479		

Personal Time

Last week we looked at the story of the rebuilding of the temple. Perhaps you were challenged to continue to pursue the Lord's plans in the face of opposition.

This week before your Group Time and your weekend worship experience, spend time using the Personal Time section of your study guide to allow the story of Esther to take root in your heart.

KNOW THE STORY

Before reading Chapter 20 of *The Story*, answer the questions below to test your knowledge of this week's Scripture. Enter your answers in the column marked "1st Time."

Question	1st Time	2nd Time
1		
2		
3		
4		

1. How did Esther become queen?
    a. The old queen was banished for disobeying the king.
    b. She was chosen by a search throughout the kingdom for beautiful girls.
    c. She pleased the king.
    d. All of the above.

2. Who plans to bring about the destruction of the Jews?
    a. Xerxes
    b. Haman
    c. Mordecai
    d. Vashti

3. How did Haman come to destruction?
    a. The king cut off his head for treason.
    b. He was killed in battle outside of Susa.
    c. He was impaled on a pole he had prepared for Mordecai's death.
    d. Mordecai stabbed him with a sword.

4. What Jewish celebration continues to this day from the story of Esther?
    a. Purim
    b. The Feast of Tabernacles
    c. Passover
    d. Pentecost

Now read Chapter 20 of *The Story*. After reading, revisit the questions to check your answers. Put your new answers in the column marked "2nd Time." (The answer key is found at the end of the session.)

UNDERSTAND THE STORY

As you read Chapter 20 of *The Story* during the week, allow the story of Esther to help you see the Lord's perfect timing and plans.

1. How do you see the Lord working through Esther's circumstances and character in the process of becoming queen?

2. How would you describe Mordecai based on his actions and words toward Haman, God, and Esther?

3. What are some of the ironies found in the downfall of Haman?

4. How did the Lord deliver his people even when the king's edict was not revoked?

5. After reading Chapter 20, what is one question you wish you could ask God about what you have read?

_____

_____

_____

_____

_____

LIVE THE STORY

TAKE ACTION

We don't want to simply be hearers of the Word but also doers of the Word. Take some time to reflect on what you have read and studied this week.

1. Did you have a new discovery from your reading and study this week? If so, what was it?

_____

_____

_____

_____

2. Is there something you need to do based on what you learned?

_____

_____

_____

_____

3. Who can you tell about what you learned? Make a plan right now to share with that person.

_____

_____

_____

_____

---------------------**TELL THE STORY**---------------------

This is our last week to focus on Movement 4. Read Movement 4 several times, filling in the blanks until you have it committed to memory. Then see if you can say all of Movement 4 without looking.

∞ Movement 4: The Story of the Church (Acts–Jude)

_____ who comes into a relationship with God through _____ in Christ belongs to the new _____ God is building called the _____. The church is commissioned to be the _____ of Christ in the Lower Story — telling his story by the way we live and the words we speak. Every story of the _____ points people to the _____ coming of Christ, when he will return to restore God's original _____.

CONVERSATION

One day around a meal or your dinner table, have an intentional conversation about this week's topic. During the meal, read Esther 4:14 found at the beginning of this session. Use the following question for discussion:

> What are examples of how God has placed us in the right time, place, or position to be involved in his plans?

PRAY TOGETHER

Focusing the last thoughts of our day on God can help us rest — truly rest — in him. Each night read and reflect on Esther 4:14, either on your own or with others if there are others living in your home. Pray and ask God to help you fully embrace the story of Esther. As you do this each night before bed, let the power of the verse impact both heart and mind.

● ● ●

Group Time

Welcome

Welcome to Session 20 of *The Story*. If there are any new members in your group, take time for introductions. You might open with a brief prayer asking God to help you understand and embrace the story of Esther.

KNOW THE STORY

Use one or both of these questions before you watch the video together.

1. How did you do on the quiz in the Know the Story section before you read the chapter?

   _____

   _____

   _____

2. What was your most interesting insight or question from your Personal Time this week?

   _____

   _____

   _____

UNDERSTAND THE STORY

As you watch the video for Session 20 of The Story, *use the section below to record some of the main points. (The answer key is found at the end of the session.)*

- Haman _____ Mordecai.

- In the Lower Story, the dice did not fall in Israel's _____.

- "And who knows but that you have come to this royal _____ for such a time as this?"

- The pole that was meant for Mordecai was now used on _____.

- People roll the dice, but God _____ how the dice will fall.

———————————LIVE THE STORY———————————

TAKE ACTION

1. What part of Randy's teaching encouraged or challenged you the most? Why?

_____

_____

_____

2. Did anything from your Personal Time jump out, calling you to action? Did anyone have an "aha" moment?

_____

_____

_____

CONVERSATION

Have someone in your group read aloud the Case Study below and then discuss the questions that follow.

> Steve had just about quit his job four months ago after eight years with the company. His boss had changed so many things the past two years, and they were more than just processes or procedures. The company philosophy had shifted, and the things they were doing now with clients bordered somewhere between dishonest and unethical. Three months ago they hired Miguel. Steve and Miguel struck up a friendship when each discovered the other was a follower of Christ. Tomorrow Miguel was going in for his three-month review. Their boss placed a huge value on "fresh eyes," and he was open to a lot of input at these three-month reviews. Today, Steve and Miguel were having lunch to talk about tomorrow's review.

1. What do you think Steve should say or not say at today's lunch?

2. Based on what you read and learned this week, how do you think Miguel should prepare for the meeting?

TELL THE STORY

As we go through *The Story* together, we want to learn how to tell the story. This is our last week to focus on Movement 4. Read Movement 4 aloud together, filling in the blanks as you commit it to memory. Then see if you can say it together as a group without looking.

✦ Movement 4: The Story of the Church (Acts–Jude)

_____ who comes into a relationship with God through _____ in Christ belongs to the new _____ God is building called the _____. The church is commissioned to be the _____ of Christ in the Lower Story — telling his story by the way we live and the words we speak. Every story of the _____ points people to the _____ coming of Christ, when he will return to restore God's original _____.

PRAY TOGETHER

One of the most important things we can do together in community is to pray for each other and those around us. Review your prayer requests from last week, and look for ways God has answered the prayers of your group. Then use the space below to record prayer requests and praises for this week. Also, make sure to pray by name for people God might add to your group — especially your neighbors.

Name   *Request/Praise*

_____   _____

_____   _____

_____   _____

_____   _____

NEXT WEEK

Next week we'll look at the story of Nehemiah and how God brings his people to rebuild the walls of the great city of Jerusalem.

Know the Story Answer Key — d / b / c / a

Video Notes Answer Key — loathes / favor / position / Haman / determines

Rebuilding the Walls

> " 'I will send my messenger, who will prepare the way before me. Then suddenly the Lord you are seeking will come to his temple; the messenger of the covenant, whom you desire, will come,' says the LORD Almighty."
>
> MALACHI 3:1

Second return of exiles	Last exiles return	Opposition to rebuilding the wall	Jerusalem's wall rebuilt	Malachi's ministry
BC 458	445		445	440–430

Personal Time

Last week we looked at the story of Esther. Perhaps God's perfect timing in fulfilling his plans for his people encouraged you.

This week before your Group Time and your weekend worship experience, spend time using the Personal Time section of your study guide to allow the stories of Ezra and Nehemiah rebuilding the walls to take root in your heart.

-------------------KNOW THE STORY-------------------

Before reading Chapter 21 of *The Story*, answer the questions below to test your knowledge of this week's Scripture. Enter your answers in the column marked "1st Time."

Question	1st Time	2nd Time
1		
2		
3		
4		

1. What was Ezra's primary role in leading the people in Jerusalem?
   a. He was the commander of their army.
   b. He was their chief builder of the temple.
   c. He was their priest and teacher.
   d. He was their chief builder of the walls.

2. What was Nehemiah's strategy for defending the city against attack?
   a. He trained an army as his first priority.
   b. He stationed the people by families along the wall.
   c. He made an alliance with Samaria to provide armed protectors.
   d. He posted signs indicating Persia's king protected the city.

3. What did Nehemiah say was the people's "strength"?
   a. The joy of the Lord.
   b. The finished walls of the city.
   c. The sword of the Lord.
   d. All of the above.

4. What does Malachi say we are doing when we withhold our tithes and offerings?
   a. We are being greedy.
   b. We are acting selfishly.
   c. We are misunderstanding money.
   d. We are robbing God.

Now read Chapter 21 of *The Story*. After reading, revisit the questions to check your answers. Put your new answers in the column marked "2nd Time." (The answer key is found at the end of the session.)

──────────────── UNDERSTAND THE STORY ────────────────

As you read Chapter 21 of *The Story* during the week, allow the stories of Ezra and Nehemiah rebuilding the walls to help you see God's Upper Story plans for Israel.

1. How did God bring favor to Israel through Ezra's actions with the people?

_____

_____

_____

_____

_____

2. Why do you think Nehemiah's strategy for defense could be so effective?

_____

_____

_____

_____

_____

3. Describe the scene of worship when Ezra read the Law. How does this challenge you regarding worship today?

_____

_____

_____

_____

_____

4. How does Malachi's warning regarding tithes and offerings challenge you?

_____

_____

_____

_____

_____

5. After reading Chapter 21, what is one question you wish you could ask God about what you have read?

LIVE THE STORY

TAKE ACTION

We don't want to simply be hearers of the Word but also doers of the Word. Take some time to reflect on what you have read and studied this week.

1. Did you have a new discovery from your reading and study this week? If so, what was it?

2. Is there something you need to do based on what you learned?

3. Who can you tell about what you learned? Make a plan right now to share with that person.

---**TELL THE STORY**---

As we go through *The Story* together, we want to learn how to tell the story. This week we will begin to focus on Movement 5. Read Movement 5 below several times as you begin to commit it to memory.

Movement 5: The Story of a New Garden (Revelation)

God will one day create a new earth and a new garden and once again come down to be with us. All who placed their faith in Christ in this life will be eternal residents in the life to come.

CONVERSATION

One day around a meal or your dinner table, have an intentional conversation about this week's topic. During the meal, read Malachi 3:1 found at the beginning of this session. Use the following question for discussion:

> How does God's promise in this verse give us hope?

PRAY TOGETHER

Focusing the last thoughts of our day on God can help us rest — truly rest — in him. Each night read and reflect on Malachi 3:1, either on your own or with others if there are others living in your home. Pray and ask God to help you fully embrace the stories of Ezra and Nehemiah..As you do this each night before bed, let the power of the verse impact both heart and mind.

● ● ●

Group Time

Welcome

Welcome to Session 21 of *The Story*. If there are any new members in your group, take time for introductions. You might open with a brief prayer asking God to help you understand and embrace the stories of Ezra and Nehemiah rebuilding the walls of Jerusalem.

KNOW THE STORY

Use one or both of these questions before you watch the video together.

1. How did you do on the quiz in the Know the Story section before you read the chapter?

2. What was your most interesting insight or question from your Personal Time this week?

UNDERSTAND THE STORY

As you watch the video for Session 21 of The Story, *use the section below to record some of the main points. (The answer key is found at the end of the session.)*

- The people are initiating their own _____ with God.
- And as he (Ezra) opened it, the people all _____.
- And their _____ was very great.
- "Prepare the way for the _____. Make straight paths for him."
- We each have the opportunity to overturn Adam's _____.

———————————LIVE THE STORY———————————

TAKE ACTION

1. What part of Randy's teaching encouraged or challenged you the most? Why?

2. Did anything from your Personal Time jump out, calling you to action? Did anyone have an "aha" moment?

CONVERSATION

Use one or two of the questions below (depending on time) to have a conversation in community.

1. As you read the description of Nehemiah rebuilding the walls, what part of the story made the biggest impact on you?

2. How does the way Ezra leads the people in worship and celebration challenge your experience of modern worship in the church?

3. How do Malachi's words related to tithes and offerings challenge you personally? Why is this often such a challenging area of obedience for followers of Jesus?

4. As you reflect on what you learned this week in Chapter 21, what is your biggest takeaway?

_____

_____

_____

TELL THE STORY

As we go through *The Story* together, we want to learn how to tell the story. This week we will begin our focus on Movement 5. Read Movement 5 aloud together to begin to commit it to memory.

Movement 5: The Story of a New Garden (Revelation)

God will one day create a new earth and a new garden and once again come down to be with us. All who placed their faith in Christ in this life will be eternal residents in the life to come.

PRAY TOGETHER

One of the most important things we can do together in community is to pray for each other and those around us. Review your prayer requests from last week, and look for ways God has answered the prayers of your group. Then use the space below to record prayer requests and praises for this week. Also, make sure to pray by name for people God might add to your group — especially your neighbors.

Name   *Request/Praise*

_____   _____

_____   _____

_____   _____

_____   _____

NEXT WEEK

Next week we'll look at the story of the birth of the King as we shift our focus to the New Testament story.

Know the Story Answer Key — c / b / a / d

Video Notes Answer Key — restoration / stood up / joy / Lord / choice

The Birth of the King

"My soul glorifies the Lord and my spirit rejoices in God my Savior, for he has been mindful of the humble state of his servant."

LUKE 1:46 – 48

Jesus is born	Flight to Egypt	Jesus visits the temple
6/5 BC	5/4 BC	AD 7/8

Personal Time

Last week we looked at the stories of Ezra and Nehemiah. Perhaps seeing God's provision and blessing in the Lower Story encouraged you.

This week before your Group Time and your weekend worship experience, spend time using the Personal Time section of your study guide to allow the story of Jesus' birth to take root in your heart.

-----------------------------KNOW THE STORY-----------------------------

Before reading Chapter 22 of *The Story*, answer the questions below to test your knowledge of this week's Scripture. Enter your answers in the column marked "1st Time."

Question	1st Time	2nd Time
1		
2		
3		
4		

1. How does John describe Jesus in his opening chapter?
   a. He calls Jesus the King.
   b. He calls Jesus the Word.
   c. He calls Jesus the Messiah.
   d. All of the above.

2. When Joseph discovered Mary was pregnant, what was his initial plan?
   a. He planned to divorce her quietly.
   b. He determined to find the man responsible.
   c. He decided to bring her before the priests for punishment.
   d. He immediately began to defend his own name with his family.

3. How many wise men from the east came to worship Jesus?
   a. Two
   b. Three
   c. Four
   d. The Bible doesn't say.

4. When Jesus stayed behind in Jerusalem at age twelve, what was he doing?
   a. He was staying with relatives for a festival.
   b. He was with the authorities because he had been left behind.
   c. He was talking with the teachers in the temple.
   d. He was hiding from his parents.

Now read Chapter 22 of *The Story*. After reading, revisit the questions to check your answers. Put your new answers in the column marked "2nd Time." (The answer key is found at the end of the session.)

---UNDERSTAND THE STORY---

As you read Chapter 22 of *The Story* during the week, allow the story of Jesus' birth to help you clearly see God's Upper Story plans coming to fruition.

1. Which part of John's description of Jesus on pages 309 and 310 inspires you the most? Why?

   _____

   _____

   _____

   _____

2. What do we learn about Joseph through his encounter with the angel and his response to this divine message?

   _____

   _____

   _____

   _____

3. What are the roles of angels in the Lower Story narrative of Jesus' birth?

   _____

   _____

   _____

   _____

4. Why do you think the authors of the Bible included only this story from Jesus' childhood?

   _____

   _____

   _____

   _____

5. After reading Chapter 22, what is one question you wish you could ask God about what you have read?

_____

_____

_____

_____

_____

———————————————LIVE THE STORY———————————————

TAKE ACTION

We don't want to simply be hearers of the Word but also doers of the Word. Take some time to reflect on what you have read and studied this week.

1. Did you have a new discovery from your reading and study this week? If so, what was it?

_____

_____

_____

_____

2. Is there something you need to do based on what you learned?

_____

_____

_____

_____

3. Who can you tell about what you learned? Make a plan right now to share with that person.

_____

_____

_____

_____

TELL THE STORY

As we go through *The Story* together, we want to learn how to tell the story. This week we will continue to focus on Movement 5. Read Movement 5 below several times as you continue to commit it to memory.

○ Movement 5: The Story of a New Garden (Revelation)

God will one day create a new earth and a new _____ and once again come down to be with us. All who placed their faith in _____ in this life will be eternal residents in the life to come.

CONVERSATION

One day around a meal or your dinner table, have an intentional conversation about this week's topic. During the meal, read Luke 1:46 – 48 found at the beginning of this session. Use the following question for discussion:

> What are specific things for which we can give God praise today? Share them, and then let's offer God thanks through simple prayers saying, "Thank you, God, for ..."

PRAY TOGETHER

Focusing the last thoughts of our day on God can help us rest — truly rest — in him. Each night read and reflect on Luke 1:46 – 48, either on your own or with others if there are others living in your home. Pray and ask God to help you fully embrace the story of the birth of Jesus. As you do this each night before bed, let the power of the verses impact both heart and mind.

● ● ●

Group Time

Welcome

Welcome to Session 22 of *The Story*. If there are any new members in your group, take time for introductions. You might open with a brief prayer asking God to help you understand and embrace the story of the birth of Jesus.

KNOW THE STORY

Use one or both of these questions before you watch the video together.

1. How did you do on the quiz in the Know the Story section before you read the chapter?

   _____

   _____

   _____

2. What was your most interesting insight or question from your Personal Time this week?

   _____

   _____

   _____

UNDERSTAND THE STORY

As you watch the video for Session 22 of The Story, *use the section below to record some of the main points. (The answer key is found at the end of the session.)*

- "She will give birth to a son, and you are to give him the name Jesus, because he will save his people from their _____."

- We learn from the Upper Story that he has been conceived _____ sin.

- Emmanuel means "God _____ us."
- _____ ruled the Lower Story.
- His birth is not the result of a scandal but a _____ to our scandal.

—LIVE THE STORY—

TAKE ACTION

1. What part of Randy's teaching encouraged or challenged you the most? Why?

   _____

   _____

   _____

2. Did anything from your Personal Time jump out, calling you to action? Did anyone have an "aha" moment?

   _____

   _____

   _____

CONVERSATION

Have someone in your group read aloud the Case Study below and then discuss the questions that follow.

Joy and Brenda were neighbors and had been building a great friendship over the past two years. The topic of faith had come up several times, and Brenda was becoming more curious about Joy's beliefs. In a blunt moment, Brenda said, "Okay, I have to be honest. There are two things about the story of Jesus as a child I don't think I could ever believe. Virgin birth? I mean, come on, Joy. You're a woman. You know that couldn't have happened. That's one. The second might be even more unbelievable. We're both moms of young children. Jesus didn't sin? Really? You've got to be kidding me! My kids didn't have to be taught to be selfish or to have tantrums or to hit each other. We didn't ever teach them the word, 'Mine.' I can't see any kid going through the early childhood years without sin!"

1. How can Joy address Brenda's legitimate struggles without jeopardizing the growing friendship God has given them?

2. Based on what you read and learned this week, how might Joy point to answers for the two questions Brenda has posed?

————————————TELL THE STORY————————————

As we go through *The Story* together, we want to learn how to tell the story. This week we will continue our focus on Movement 5. Read Movement 5 aloud together to continue to commit it to memory.

🔑 Movement 5: The Story of a New Garden (Revelation)

God will one day create a new earth and a new _____ and once again come down to be with us. All who placed their faith in _____ in this life will be eternal residents in the life to come.

PRAY TOGETHER

One of the most important things we can do together in community is to pray for each other and those around us. Review your prayer requests from last week, and look for ways God has answered the prayers of your group. Then use the space below to record prayer requests and praises for this week. Also, make sure to pray by name for people God might add to your group — especially your neighbors.

Name   *Request/Praise*

_____   _____

_____   _____

_____   _____

_____   _____

————————————NEXT WEEK————————————

Next week we'll look at the story of the beginning of Jesus' surprisingly quiet entry into the public part of his earthly ministry.

Know the Story Answer Key — b / a / d / c

Video Notes Answer Key — sins / without / with / Caesar / solution

Jesus' Ministry Begins

"As soon as Jesus was baptized, he went up
out of the water. At that moment heaven
was opened, and he saw the Spirit of God
descending like a dove and alighting on him.
And a voice from heaven said, 'This is my Son,
whom I love; with him I am well pleased.'"

MATTHEW 3:16–17

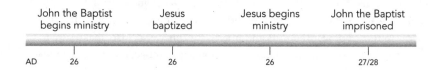

John the Baptist begins ministry	Jesus baptized	Jesus begins ministry	John the Baptist imprisoned
AD 26	26	26	27/28

Personal Time

Last week we looked at the story of the birth of Jesus. Perhaps you were encouraged by the Lower Story details of Jesus' birth helping to fulfill God's Upper Story plans to restore his people.

This week before your Group Time and your weekend worship experience, spend time using the Personal Time section of your study guide to allow the story of Jesus' early ministry to take root in your heart.

KNOW THE STORY

Before reading Chapter 23 of *The Story*, answer the questions below to test your knowledge of this week's Scripture. Enter your answers in the column marked "1st Time."

Question	1st Time	2nd Time
1		
2		
3		
4		

1. What was Jesus' first public miracle?
    a. He touched the eyes of the man who was born blind.
    b. He healed the man from Galilee who had leprosy.
    c. He turned water into wine.
    d. He gave the early disciples a huge catch of fish.

2. According to Jesus' words to the woman at the well, how will true worshipers worship?
    a. They will worship with loud voices and singing.
    b. They will worship in Spirit and in truth.
    c. They will worship with hands lifted high in praise.
    d. They will worship in deeds of service to the poor.

3. What was Nicodemus's role when he came to meet with Jesus in the night?
    a. He was one of the twelve disciples.
    b. He was a tax collector.
    c. He was the chief priest.
    d. He was a member of the Jewish ruling council.

4. What did Jesus say when the lame man was lowered by friends through the roof?
    a. "Your sins are forgiven."
    b. "I have never seen such faith in all of Israel."
    c. "Your faith has made you well."
    d. "Do you want to be healed?"

Now read Chapter 23 of *The Story*. After reading, revisit the questions to check your answers. Put your new answers in the column marked "2nd Time." (The answer key is found at the end of the session.)

UNDERSTAND THE STORY

As you read Chapter 23 of *The Story* during the week, allow the story of Jesus' early ministry help you gain a greater understanding of the Lower Story of Jesus.

1. What do you think is the significance of Jesus' baptism experience?

2. Why do you think Jesus chose to reveal his identity to the woman at the well?

3. How did Jesus use healings and miracles to advance his ministry and message?

4. Put yourself in the sandals of John the Baptist. How would you have responded to the answer Jesus gave to John's disciples?

5. After reading Chapter 23, what is one question you wish you could ask God about what you have read?

_____

_____

_____

_____

─────LIVE THE STORY─────

TAKE ACTION

We don't want to simply be hearers of the Word but also doers of the Word. Take some time to reflect on what you have read and studied this week.

1. Did you have a new discovery from your reading and study this week? If so, what was it?

_____

_____

_____

_____

2. Is there something you need to do based on what you learned?

_____

_____

_____

_____

3. Who can you tell about what you learned? Make a plan right now to share with that person.

_____

_____

_____

_____

TELL THE STORY

As we go through *The Story* together, we want to learn how to tell the story. This week we will continue to focus on Movement 5. Read Movement 5 below several times as you continue to commit it to memory.

🔑 Movement 5: The Story of a New Garden (Revelation)

God will one day create a new _____ and a new _____ and once again come down to be with us. All who placed their faith in _____ in this life will be _____ residents in the life to come.

CONVERSATION

One day around a meal or your dinner table, have an intentional conversation about this week's topic. During the meal, read Matthew 3:16 – 17 found at the beginning of this session. Use the following question for discussion:

> Why would it be important for Jesus to hear his Father's blessing?

PRAY TOGETHER

Focusing the last thoughts of our day on God can help us rest — truly rest — in him. Each night read and reflect on Matthew 3:16 – 17, either on your own or with others if there are others living in your home. Pray and ask God to help you fully embrace the story of Jesus' early ministry. As you do this each night before bed, let the power of the verses impact both heart and mind.

● ● ●

Group Time

Welcome

Welcome to Session 23 of *The Story*. If there are any new members in your group, take time for introductions. You might open with a brief prayer asking God to help you understand and embrace the stories of Jesus' early ministry.

KNOW THE STORY

Use one or both of these questions before you watch the video together.

1. How did you do on the quiz in the Know the Story section before you read the chapter?

2. What was your most interesting insight or question from your Personal Time this week?

UNDERSTAND THE STORY

As you watch the video for Session 23 of The Story, *use the section below to record some of the main points. (The answer key is found at the end of the session.)*

- John is going to tell us that the solution is not a "what" but a "_____."

- "Look, the _____ of God, who takes away the sin of the world!"

- Jesus is the "who" we have been _____ for.

- "I, the one _____ to you—I am he."

- The God of the Upper Story entered into the Lower Story to provide the final _____ to our grandest problem. His name is Jesus.

LIVE THE STORY

TAKE ACTION

1. What part of Randy's teaching encouraged or challenged you the most? Why?

2. Did anything from your Personal Time jump out, calling you to action? Did anyone have an "aha" moment?

CONVERSATION

Use one or two of the questions below (depending on time) to have a conversation in community.

1. Why did Jesus choose to be baptized? What does this teach us about the importance of baptism?

2. Which part of Jesus' exchange with either Nicodemus or the woman at the well has the most significance to you? Why?

3. Jesus performed several miracles and healings. How did he use these encounters to advance his early ministry?

4. As you reflect on what you learned this week in Chapter 23, what is your biggest takeaway?

_____

_____

_____

TELL THE STORY

As we go through *The Story* together, we want to learn how to tell the story. This week we will continue our focus on Movement 5. Read Movement 5 aloud together to continue to commit it to memory.

✜ Movement 5: The Story of a New Garden (Revelation)

God will one day create a new _____ and a new _____ and once again come down to be with us. All who placed their faith in _____ in this life will be _____ residents in the life to come.

PRAY TOGETHER

One of the most important things we can do together in community is to pray for each other and those around us. Review your prayer requests from last week, and look for ways God has answered the prayers of your group. Then use the space below to record prayer requests and praises for this week. Also, make sure to pray by name for people God might add to your group — especially your neighbors.

Name   *Request/Praise*

_____   _____

_____   _____

_____   _____

_____   _____

NEXT WEEK

Next week we'll look at the stories of Jesus' growing public ministry as he encounters larger and larger crowds.

Know the Story Answer Key — c / b / d / a

Video Notes Answer Key — who / Lamb / waiting / speaking / solution

No Ordinary Man

"I am the vine; you are the branches. If you remain in me and I in you, you will bear much fruit; apart from me you can do nothing."

JOHN 15:5

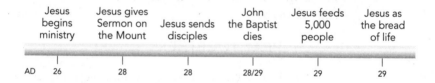

Jesus begins ministry	Jesus gives Sermon on the Mount	Jesus sends disciples	John the Baptist dies	Jesus feeds 5,000 people	Jesus as the bread of life
AD 26	28	28	28/29	29	29

Personal Time

Last week we looked at the story of Jesus' early ministry. Perhaps you were amazed by the way Jesus used miracles and healings in so many lives.

This week before your Group Time and your weekend worship experience, spend time using the Personal Time section of your study guide to allow the stories of Jesus' growing popularity to take root in your heart.

KNOW THE STORY

Before reading Chapter 24 of *The Story*, answer the questions below to test your knowledge of this week's Scripture. Enter your answers in the column marked "1st Time."

Question	1st Time	2nd Time
1		
2		
3		
4		

1. Which one of the following is NOT a parable of Jesus?
    a. The parable of the prodigal son
    b. The parable of the lost coin
    c. The parable of the stubborn donkey
    d. The parable of the lost sheep

2. The Beatitudes are the statements beginning with "Blessed are." What statement is NOT included in the Beatitudes?
    a. Blessed are the discerning.
    b. Blessed are those who mourn.
    c. Blessed are the peacemakers.
    d. Blessed are the meek.

3. When Jesus cast the legion of demons out, where did he send the demons?
    a. He sent them into eternal exile.
    b. He sent them into a herd of pigs.
    c. He sent them into the Abyss.
    d. He sent them into a barren wilderness.

4. What did Jesus and his disciples use to feed the crowd of five thousand?
    a. Twelve loaves of bread and twelve fish
    b. Twelve baskets full of bread and fish
    c. Five fish and two loaves of bread
    d. Five loaves of bread and two fish

Now read Chapter 24 of *The Story*. After reading, revisit the questions to check your answers. Put your new answers in the column marked "2nd Time." (The answer key is found at the end of the session.)

UNDERSTAND THE STORY

As you read Chapter 24 of *The Story* during the week, allow the stories of Jesus' teachings on the kingdom help you gain a greater understanding of the heart of Jesus.

1. After reading the three parables about the lost things, how would you describe God's heart toward you?

2. Which part of the Sermon on the Mount provides you the greatest challenge? Which part provides you the greatest encouragement?

3. In the two encounters the disciples had with Jesus on the water, what were some of the things he wanted them to learn and know?

4. What do you think it was about Jesus' teaching that drew large crowds? What do you think it was about Jesus' teaching that caused people to turn away? How is this similar in the church today?

5. After reading Chapter 24, what is one question you wish you could ask God about what you have read?

_____

_____

_____

_____

―――――――――――――**LIVE THE STORY**―――――――――――――

TAKE ACTION

We don't want to simply be hearers of the Word but also doers of the Word. Take some time to reflect on what you have read and studied this week.

1. Did you have a new discovery from your reading and study this week? If so, what was it?

_____

_____

_____

_____

2. Is there something you need to do based on what you learned?

_____

_____

_____

_____

3. Who can you tell about what you learned? Make a plan right now to share with that person.

_____

_____

_____

_____

TELL THE STORY

As we go through *The Story* together, we want to learn how to tell the story. This week we will continue to focus on Movement 5. Read Movement 5 below several times as you continue to commit it to memory.

Movement 5: The Story of a New Garden (Revelation)

_____ will one day create a new _____ and a new _____ and once again come down to be _____ us. All who placed their faith in _____ in this life will be _____ residents in the life to come.

CONVERSATION

One day around a meal or your dinner table, have an intentional conversation about this week's topic. During the meal, read John 15:5 found at the beginning of this session. Use the following question for discussion:

What are specific ways we stay connected to Jesus as the vine?

PRAY TOGETHER

Focusing the last thoughts of our day on God can help us rest — truly rest — in him. Each night read and reflect on John 15:5, either on your own or with others if there are others living in your home. Pray and ask God to help you fully embrace the stories of Jesus' power. As you do this each night before bed, let the power of the verse impact both heart and mind.

● ● ●

Group Time

Welcome

Welcome to Session 24 of *The Story*. If there are any new members in your group, take time for introductions. You might open with a brief prayer asking God to help you understand and embrace the stories of Jesus' teachings and miracles.

KNOW THE STORY

Use one or both of these questions before you watch the video together.

1. How did you do on the quiz in the Know the Story section before you read the chapter?

   _____

   _____

   _____

2. What was your most interesting insight or question from your Personal Time this week?

   _____

   _____

   _____

UNDERSTAND THE STORY

As you watch the video for Session 24 of The Story, *use the section below to record some of the main points. (The answer key is found at the end of the session.)*

- "He who has ears to hear, let him _____."
- The kingdom of God is that restored _____.
- "Our Father in heaven, Hallowed be your _____."
- We cry out to God to meet us in our _____ Story.
- If you want to walk on water, you need to concentrate on walking _____ Jesus.

---LIVE THE STORY---

TAKE ACTION

1. What part of Randy's teaching encouraged or challenged you the most? Why?

2. Did anything from your Personal Time jump out, calling you to action? Did anyone have an "aha" moment?

CONVERSATION

Have someone in your group read aloud the Case Study below and then discuss the questions that follow.

Everyone in the department knew Don was a follower of Christ. One of his coworkers, John, also attended church, but he had a different perspective on personal faith. John and Don were having a conversation one day about their week when John said to Don, "I know you take everything about church and Jesus seriously. I think the most important thing in life is to have balance. You need a little bit of work, a little bit of family, and a little bit of church. If any one of those things gets to be too important or takes up too much of your focus, you get out of balance. That's when you start to have problems. My goal is always balance."

1. What do you think about John's statement regarding balance?

2. Based on what you read and learned about Jesus' life and ministry this week, how might Don respond to John?

TELL THE STORY

As we go through *The Story* together, we want to learn how to tell the story. This week we will continue our focus on Movement 5. Read Movement 5 aloud together to continue to commit it to memory.

Movement 5: The Story of a New Garden (Revelation)

_____ will one day create a new _____ and a new _____ and once again come down to be _____ us. All who placed their faith in _____ in this life will be _____ residents in the life to come.

PRAY TOGETHER

One of the most important things we can do together in community is to pray for each other and those around us. Review your prayer requests from last week, and look for ways God has answered the prayers of your group. Then use the space below to record prayer requests and praises for this week. Also, make sure to pray by name for people God might add to your group — especially your neighbors.

Name   *Request/Praise*

_____   _____

_____   _____

_____   _____

_____   _____

NEXT WEEK

Next week we'll look at the story of Jesus leading up to his betrayal by Judas.

Know the Story Answer Key — c / a / b / d

Video Notes Answer Key — hear / garden / name / Lower / toward

Jesus, the Son of God

"I am the way and the truth and the
life. No one comes to the Father except
through me. If you really know me, you
will know my Father as well. From now on,
you do know him and have seen him."

JOHN 14:6 – 7

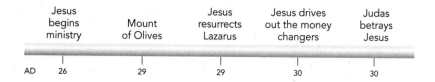

	Jesus begins ministry	Mount of Olives	Jesus resurrects Lazarus	Jesus drives out the money changers	Judas betrays Jesus
AD	26	29	29	30	30

Personal Time

Last week we looked at the stories of Jesus' growing public ministry. Perhaps
you were inspired to see the heart and power of Jesus more clearly.

This week before your Group Time and your weekend worship experience,
spend time using the Personal Time section of your study guide to allow the
story of the last season of Jesus' life to take root in your heart.

KNOW THE STORY

Before reading Chapter 25 of *The Story*, answer the questions below to test your knowledge of this week's Scripture. Enter your answers in the column marked "1st Time."

Question	1st Time	2nd Time
1		
2		
3		
4		

1. Who appeared with Jesus on the Mount of Transfiguration?
    a. Two angels
    b. Abraham and Isaac
    c. Moses and Elijah
    d. Jeremiah and Ezekiel

2. How many days was Lazarus in the tomb before Jesus raised him from the dead?
    a. 4 days
    b. 3 days
    c. 2 days
    d. 1 day

3. What did the crowds shout when Jesus entered Jerusalem?
    a. "Behold the Lamb of God who takes away the sin of the world!"
    b. "Blessed is he who comes in the name of the Lord!"
    c. "Worthy is the Lamb to receive all glory, honor, and praise!"
    d. "Crucify him! Crucify him!"

4. What claims did Jesus make about himself?
    a. "I am from above."
    b. "I am the light of the world."
    c. "I am the resurrection and the life."
    d. All of the above.

Now read Chapter 25 of *The Story*. After reading, revisit the questions to check your answers. Put your new answers in the column marked "2nd Time." (The answer key is found at the end of the session.)

UNDERSTAND THE STORY

As you read Chapter 25 of *The Story* during the week, allow the stories of Jesus' growing power and influence to help you see his true identity more clearly.

1. What do you think Jesus was hoping to demonstrate to Peter, James, and John on the Mount of Transfiguration?

2. Although Jesus performed many miracles, he did not heal everyone. Why do you suppose Jesus raised Lazarus from the dead, but he didn't raise others?

3. As Jesus entered Jerusalem, what do you believe were the hopes people had for him? What do you think they wanted most and why?

4. How could the crowds have shifted their attitude toward Jesus in such a short time? How are the Lower Story circumstances clouding their view of the Upper Story?

5. After reading Chapter 25, what is one question you wish you could ask God about what you have read?

_____

_____

_____

_____

_____

LIVE THE STORY

TAKE ACTION

We don't want to simply be hearers of the Word but also doers of the Word. Take some time to reflect on what you have read and studied this week.

1. Did you have a new discovery from your reading and study this week? If so, what was it?

_____

_____

_____

_____

_____

2. Is there something you need to do based on what you learned?

_____

_____

_____

_____

_____

3. Who can you tell about what you learned? Make a plan right now to share with that person.

_____

_____

_____

_____

_____

TELL THE STORY

This is our last week to focus on Movement 5. Read Movement 5 below several times, filling in the blanks until you have it committed to memory. Then see if you can say all of Movement 5 without looking.

○ Movement 5: The Story of a New Garden (Revelation)

_____ will one day create a new _____ and a new _____ and once again come down to be _____ us. All who placed their _____ in _____ in this life will be _____ residents in the _____ to come.

CONVERSATION

One day around a meal or your dinner table, have an intentional conversation about this week's topic. During the meal, read John 14:6 – 7 found at the beginning of this session. Use the following question for discussion:

> What are examples of how Jesus gives us "the way, the truth, and the life"?

PRAY TOGETHER

Focusing the last thoughts of our day on God can help us rest — truly rest — in him. Each night read and reflect on John 14:6 – 7, either on your own or with others if there are others living in your home. Pray and ask God to help you fully embrace the stories of Jesus' growing impact. As you do this each night before bed, let the power of the verses impact both heart and mind.

● ● ●

Group Time

Welcome

Welcome to Session 25 of *The Story*. If there are any new members in your group, take time for introductions. You might open with a brief prayer asking God to help you understand and embrace the stories of Jesus' earthly power and authority.

KNOW THE STORY

Use one or both of these questions before you watch the video together.

1. How did you do on the quiz in the Know the Story section before you read the chapter?

2. What was your most interesting insight or question from your Personal Time this week?

UNDERSTAND THE STORY

As you watch the video for Session 25 of The Story, *use the section below to record some of the main points. (The answer key is found at the end of the session.)*

- What's my _____?
- Peter decided to _____ Jesus.
- Jesus said, "I am the _____ of the world."
- "See your king comes to you ... gentle and riding on a _____."
- "Three days later I will _____."

---LIVE THE STORY---

TAKE ACTION

1. What part of Randy's teaching encouraged or challenged you the most? Why?

_____

_____

_____

2. Did anything from your Personal Time jump out, calling you to action? Did anyone have an "aha" moment?

_____

_____

_____

CONVERSATION

Use one or two of the questions below (depending on time) to have a conversation in community.

1. Some of the things Jesus did confused his listeners. What did you read this week about Jesus that you found confusing or challenging?

_____

_____

_____

2. Of all of the things Jesus said and did prior to dying on the cross, which convinces you most that he was God in the flesh, and why?

_____

_____

_____

3. What do you think was the religious leaders' biggest fear of Jesus? Why did they have this fear?

_____

_____

_____

4. As you reflect on what you learned this week in Chapter 25, what is your biggest takeaway?

_____

_____

_____

——————TELL THE STORY——————

As we go through *The Story* together, we want to learn how to tell the story. This is our last week to focus on Movement 5. Read Movement 5 aloud together, filling in the blanks as you commit it memory. Then see if you can say it as a group without looking.

⚓ Movement 5: The Story of a New Garden (Revelation)

_____ will one day create a new _____ and a new _____ and once again come down to be _____ us. All who placed their _____ in _____ in this life will be _____ residents in the _____ to come.

——————PRAY TOGETHER——————

One of the most important things we can do together in community is to pray for each other and those around us. Review your prayer requests from last week, and look for ways God has answered the prayers of your group. Then use the space below to record prayer requests and praises for this week. Also, make sure to pray by name for people God might add to your group — especially your neighbors.

Name   *Request/Praise*

_____   _____

_____   _____

_____   _____

——————NEXT WEEK——————

Next week we'll look at the powerful story of Jesus' death and how all of eternity was changed by this one act of sacrifice.

Know the Story Answer Key—c / a / b / d

Video Notes Answer Key—line / rebuke / light / donkey / rise

The Hour of Darkness

"Then one of the Twelve — the one called Judas Iscariot — went to the chief priests and asked, 'What are you willing to give me if I deliver him over to you?' So they counted out for him thirty pieces of silver. From then on Judas watched for an opportunity to hand him over."

MATTHEW 26:14–16

The Lord's Supper	Jesus washes disciples' feet	Jesus comforts disciples	Jesus arrested	Peter denies Jesus	Jesus crucified

AD 30

Personal Time

Last week we looked at the growing power of Jesus' public ministry. Perhaps you were challenged as you saw him reveal himself more clearly to the people.

This week before your Group Time and your weekend worship experience, spend time using the Personal Time section of your study guide to allow the story of Jesus' crucifixion to take root in your heart.

KNOW THE STORY

Before reading Chapter 26 of _The Story_, answer the questions below to test your knowledge of this week's Scripture. Enter your answers in the column marked "1st Time."

Question	1st Time	2nd Time
1		
2		
3		
4		

1. How did Jesus indicate to his disciples which disciple was going to betray him?
   a. He told them the name of the betrayer.
   b. He told them a parable about betrayal.
   c. He dipped a piece of bread toward the betrayer.
   d. He caused the betrayer to confess to them in the Upper Room.

2. What healing did Jesus do in the garden of Gethsemane?
   a. He healed a man who had been deaf since birth.
   b. He healed a man who had his ear cut off.
   c. He healed a woman of her barrenness.
   d. He healed a leper who lived in the garden.

3. Why did Pilate agree to crucify Jesus?
   a. He was trying to appease the crowd.
   b. He found Jesus guilty of the charges against him.
   c. He felt threatened when he found out Jesus was the King of the Jews.
   d. He became angry with Jesus when Jesus refused to answer his questions.

4. What were Jesus' final words before his death on the cross?
   a. "Forgive them for they know not what they do."
   b. "My God, my God, why have you forsaken me?"
   c. "Today you will be with me in paradise."
   d. "It is finished."

Now read Chapter 26 of _The Story_. After reading, revisit the questions to check your answers. Put your new answers in the column marked "2nd Time." (The answer key is found at the end of the session.)

UNDERSTAND THE STORY

As you read Chapter 26 of *The Story* during the week, allow the story of Jesus' betrayal and crucifixion to help you have a clearer picture of his amazing gift to us.

1. Put in your own words the range of emotions Jesus would have experienced in his encounter with Judas in the upper room.

    _____

    _____

    _____

    _____

    _____

2. What do you see as the main point(s) of Jesus' final prayer before he and the disciples left for the Mount of Olives?

    _____

    _____

    _____

    _____

3. Peter was so certain he would not deny Jesus. What do you think led to his denials? How do we face similar challenges in our own faith journey?

    _____

    _____

    _____

    _____

    _____

4. In your own words, describe what happened with the temple curtain in both the Lower Story and the Upper Story.

    _____

    _____

    _____

    _____

5. After reading Chapter 26, what is one question you wish you could ask God about what you have read?

_____

_____

_____

_____

_____

LIVE THE STORY

TAKE ACTION

We don't want to simply be hearers of the Word but also doers of the Word. Take some time to reflect on what you have read and studied this week.

1. Did you have a new discovery from your reading and study this week? If so, what was it?

_____

_____

_____

_____

_____

2. Is there something you need to do based on what you learned?

_____

_____

_____

_____

_____

3. Who can you tell about what you learned? Make a plan right now to share with that person.

_____

_____

_____

_____

_____

TELL THE STORY

As we have gone through *The Story* together, we have been learning how to tell the story. This week we review Movement 1. Read Movement 1 below several times to make sure you have it committed to memory.

Movement 1: The Story of the Garden (Genesis 1–11)

In the Upper Story, God creates the Lower Story. His vision is to come down and be with us in a beautiful garden. The first two people reject God's vision and are escorted from paradise. Their decision introduces sin into the human race and keeps us from community with God. At this moment God gives a promise and launches a plan to get us back. The rest of the Bible is God's story of how he kept that promise and made it possible for us to enter a loving relationship with him.

CONVERSATION

One day around a meal or your dinner table, have an intentional conversation about this week's topic. During the meal, read Matthew 26:14–16 found at the beginning of this session. Use the following questions for discussion:

> What does it feel like to have someone turn against us? How should we handle a situation like that if it occurs?

PRAY TOGETHER

Focusing the last thoughts of our day on God can help us rest — truly rest — in him. Each night read Matthew 26:14–16, either on your own or with others if there are others living in your home. Pray and ask God to help you fully embrace the story of Jesus giving his life for our sins. As you do this each night before bed, let the power of the verses impact both heart and mind.

• • •

Group Time

Welcome

Welcome to Session 25 of *The Story*. If there are any new members in your group, take time for introductions. You might open with a brief prayer asking God to help you understand and embrace the story of the cross.

KNOW THE STORY

Use one or both of these questions before you watch the video together.

1. How did you do on the quiz in the Know the Story section before you read the chapter?

   _____

   _____

   _____

2. What was your most interesting insight or question from your Personal Time this week?

   _____

   _____

   _____

UNDERSTAND THE STORY

As you watch the video for Session 26 of The Story, *use the section below to record some of the main points. (The answer key is found at the end of the session.)*

- The outcome of this event looks totally different from the _____ Story compared to the _____ Story.

- They placed a _____ robe on him as a mockery.

- "But not my will but _____ will be done."

- He was _____ for our transgressions.

- The curse of Adam has been _____.

LIVE THE STORY

TAKE ACTION

1. What part of Randy's teaching encouraged or challenged you the most? Why?

    _____

    _____

    _____

2. Did anything from your Personal Time jump out, calling you to action? Did anyone have an "aha" moment?

    _____

    _____

    _____

CONVERSATION

Have someone in your group read aloud the Case Study below and then discuss the questions that follow.

Anita poured out her heart in tears over the phone to her friend, Wendy, who lived on the other side of the country. Recently, Anita had discovered her company was involved in corporate fraud. After a month of struggling with the decision, she had decided to become a whistleblower. She felt as though she was doing the right thing, but the consequences were enormous. She had experienced death threats. Hundreds of people were losing their jobs. Families were destroyed. Even Anita's husband questioned her decision, and their marriage was strained. Her friend, Wendy, had been a spiritual mentor back when Anita was in school. Now, Anita was turning to Wendy crying out for help.

1. How should we make decisions about what to do when the potential consequences might seem overwhelming?

2. Based on what you read and learned this week, what should Wendy say to Anita?

---TELL THE STORY---

As we have gone through *The Story* together, we have been learning each week how to tell the story. This week we review Movement 1. Read it aloud together to make sure you have it committed to memory. Repeat it until the group is able to say it without looking.

 Movement 1: The Story of the Garden (Genesis 1–11)

In the Upper Story, God creates the Lower Story. His vision is to come down and be with us in a beautiful garden. The first two people reject God's vision and are escorted from paradise. Their decision introduces sin into the human race and keeps us from community with God. At this moment God gives a promise and launches a plan to get us back. The rest of the Bible is God's story of how he kept that promise and made it possible for us to enter a loving relationship with him.

---PRAY TOGETHER---

One of the most important things we can do together in community is to pray for each other and those around us. Review your prayer requests from last week, and look for ways God has answered the prayers of your group. Then use the space below to record prayer requests and praises for this week. Also, make sure to pray by name for people God might add to your group—especially your neighbors.

Name   *Request/Praise*

_____   _____

_____   _____

_____   _____

_____   _____

---NEXT WEEK---

Next week we'll look at the story of the amazing resurrection of Jesus and how he had power over death.

Know the Story Answer Key — c / b / a / d

Video Notes Answer Key — Lower / Upper / purple / your / pierced / lifted

The Resurrection

"You are looking for Jesus the Nazarene, who was crucified. He has risen! He is not here. See the place where they laid him."

MARK 16:6

	Jesus buried	Jesus resurrected	Jesus appears to Mary Magdalene and the disciples

AD   30

Personal Time

Last week we looked at the story of Jesus' death on the cross. Perhaps you were challenged by the magnitude of his great sacrifice for us.

This week before your Group Time and your weekend worship experience, spend time using the Personal Time section of your study guide to allow the story of Jesus' resurrection to take root in your heart.

KNOW THE STORY

Before reading Chapter 27 of *The Story*, answer the questions below to test your knowledge of this week's Scripture. Enter your answers in the column marked "1st Time."

Question	1st Time	2nd Time
1		
2		
3		
4		

1. Who prepared Jesus' body for burial?
   a. Nicodemus
   b. Joseph of Arimathea
   c. Nicodemus and Joseph of Arimathea
   d. Neither Nicodemus nor Joseph of Arimathea

2. At the empty tomb, when did Mary know she was talking to the risen Christ?
   a. She knew when he showed her the scars on his hands.
   b. She knew when he said her name.
   c. She knew as soon as he started to talk to her.
   d. She knew when the two angels announced it to her.

3. Who was the last of the remaining eleven disciples to see Jesus alive?
   a. Thomas
   b. John
   c. Peter
   d. Nathanael

4. What question did Jesus ask Peter to attempt to restore their relationship?
   a. "What did you do wrong?"
   b. "Why did you deny me?"
   c. "Do you commit to serving me?"
   d. "Do you love me?"

Now read Chapter 27 of *The Story*. After reading, revisit the questions to check your answers. Put your new answers in the column marked "2nd Time." (The answer key is found at the end of the session.)

UNDERSTAND THE STORY

As you read Chapter 27of *The Story* during the week, allow the story of Jesus' resurrection to help you embrace the importance of his victory over death.

1. How likely do you think it was that the disciples would try to steal Jesus' body? Why do you feel this way?

_____

_____

_____

_____

2. Put yourself in the place of Mary Magdalene on resurrection morning. What was the range of emotions she experienced?

_____

_____

_____

_____

3. What do you think Jesus was trying to accomplish through the multiple appearances to the disciples after the resurrection?

_____

_____

_____

_____

4. What is the significance to you personally of Jesus' final words to the disciples on the mountain?

_____

_____

_____

_____

5. After reading Chapter 27, what is one question you wish you could ask God about what you have read?

—————————————————————————————————

—————————————————————————————————

—————————————————————————————————

—————————————————————————————————

—————————————————————————————————

LIVE THE STORY

TAKE ACTION

We don't want to simply be hearers of the Word but also doers of the Word. Take some time to reflect on what you have read and studied this week.

1. Did you have a new discovery from your reading and study this week? If so, what was it?

—————————————————————————————————

—————————————————————————————————

—————————————————————————————————

—————————————————————————————————

2. Is there something you need to do based on what you learned?

—————————————————————————————————

—————————————————————————————————

—————————————————————————————————

—————————————————————————————————

3. Who can you tell about what you learned? Make a plan right now to share with that person.

—————————————————————————————————

—————————————————————————————————

—————————————————————————————————

—————————————————————————————————

———TELL THE STORY———

As we have gone through *The Story* together, we have been learning how to tell the story. This week we review Movement 2. Read Movement 2 below several times to make sure you have it committed to memory.

Movement 2: The Story of Israel (Genesis 12–Malachi)

God builds a brand-new nation called Israel. Through this nation, he will reveal his presence, power, and plan to get us back. Every story of Israel will point to the first coming of Jesus — the One who will provide the way back to God.

CONVERSATION

One day around a meal or your dinner table, have an intentional conversation about this week's topic. During the meal, read Mark 16:6 found at the beginning of this session. Use the following question for discussion:

Why is it important for us to believe Jesus rose from the dead?

PRAY TOGETHER

Focusing the last thoughts of our day on God can help us rest — truly rest — in him. Each night read Mark 16:6, either on your own or with others if there are others living in your home. Pray and ask God to help you fully embrace the story of Jesus' miraculous resurrection. As you do this each night before bed, let the power of the verse impact both heart and mind.

● ● ●

Group Time

Welcome

Welcome to Session 27 of *The Story*. If there are any new members in your group, take time for introductions. You might open with a brief prayer asking God to help you understand and embrace the story of Jesus' resurrection.

KNOW THE STORY

Use one or both of these questions before you watch the video together.

1. How did you do on the quiz in the Know the Story section before you read the chapter?

2. What was your most interesting insight or question from your Personal Time this week?

UNDERSTAND THE STORY

As you watch the video for Session 27 of The Story, *use the section below to record some of the main points. (The answer key is found at the end of the session.)*

- There was a violent _____, for an angel of the Lord came down from heaven.

- When they got there, the _____ had already been rolled away from the tomb.

- They did not understand from _____ that Jesus had to rise from the dead.

- Jesus told us that the _____ was the place we would capture his presence the best.
- Jesus is not _____. He is alive.

—————LIVE THE STORY—————

TAKE ACTION

1. What part of Randy's teaching encouraged or challenged you the most? Why?

   _____

   _____

   _____

2. Did anything from your Personal Time jump out, calling you to action? Did anyone have an "aha" moment?

   _____

   _____

   _____

CONVERSATION

Use one or two of the questions below (depending on time) to have a conversation in community.

1. How are you encouraged or comforted by the story of Peter's restoration? How does that story relate to your own life and faith?

   _____

   _____

   _____

2. Jesus had an interaction with two men on the road to Emmaus. What is the significance of the phrase "then their eyes were opened"?

   _____

   _____

   _____

3. Why is the resurrection of Jesus absolutely critical to the Christian faith?

_____

_____

_____

_____

4. As you reflect on what you learned this week in Chapter 27, what is your biggest takeaway?

_____

_____

_____

_____

—————————TELL THE STORY—————————

As we have gone through *The Story* together, we have been learning each week how to tell the story. This week we review Movement 2. Read it aloud together to make sure you have it committed to memory. Repeat it until the group is able to say it without looking.

🕎 Movement 2: The Story of Israel (Genesis 12 – Malachi)

God builds a brand-new nation called Israel. Through this nation, he will reveal his presence, power, and plan to get us back. Every story of Israel will point to the first coming of Jesus — the One who will provide the way back to God.

—————————PRAY TOGETHER—————————

One of the most important things we can do together in community is to pray for each other and those around us. Review your prayer requests from last week, and look for ways God has answered the prayers of your group. Then use the space below to record prayer requests and praises for this week. Also, make sure to pray by name for people God might add to your group — especially your neighbors.

Name   *Request/Praise*

_____   _____

_____   _____

_____   _____

_____   _____

NEXT WEEK

Next week we'll look at the story of the beginning of the church and how rapidly God expanded the church in its early days.

Know the Story Answer Key — c / b / a / d

Video Notes Answer Key — earthquake / stone / Scripture / table / finished

New Beginnings

"All this I have spoken while still with you. But the Advocate, the Holy Spirit, whom the Father will send in my name, will teach you all things and will remind you of everything I have said to you. Peace I leave with you; my peace I give you. I do not give to you as the world gives. Do not let your hearts be troubled and do not be afraid."

JOHN 14:25 – 27

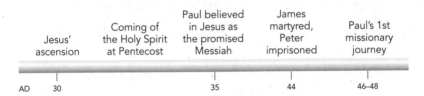

	Jesus' ascension	Coming of the Holy Spirit at Pentecost	Paul believed in Jesus as the promised Messiah	James martyred, Peter imprisoned	Paul's 1st missionary journey
AD	30		35	44	46–48

Personal Time

Last week we looked at the story of Jesus' resurrection. Perhaps the powerful evidence for his resurrection encouraged you.

This week before your Group Time and your weekend worship experience, spend time using the Personal Time section of your study guide to allow the story of the beginning of the early church to take root in your heart.

KNOW THE STORY

Before reading Chapter 28 of *The Story*, answer the questions below to test your knowledge of this week's Scripture. Enter your answers in the column marked "1st Time."

Question	1st Time	2nd Time
1		
2		
3		
4		

1. What was the evidence of the Holy Spirit's arrival at Pentecost?
   a. Tongues of fire rested on them.
   b. They spoke in different languages.
   c. There was a sound like a violent wind.
   d. All of the above.

2. What did the people hope Peter would do to heal the sick in the streets?
   a. They hoped his shadow would fall on them.
   b. They hoped he would speak words of healing to them.
   c. They hoped he would anoint them with healing oil.
   d. They hoped he would touch them with his hands and heal them.

3. What happened when Saul went to Damascus to persecute Christians?
   a. Saul had Stephen killed there.
   b. Saul was struck blind.
   c. The angel of the Lord killed Saul.
   d. Saul was prevented from entering Damascus by an angel.

4. What did Peter see in his dream prior to going to meet with Cornelius?
   a. He saw a vision of a family from another country calling to him.
   b. He saw Jesus on the cross, and Peter himself was holding the hammer.
   c. He saw a sheet with unclean animals on it that he was told to eat.
   d. He saw himself nailed to a cross upside down.

Now read Chapter 28 of *The Story*. After reading, revisit the questions to check your answers. Put your new answers in the column marked "2nd Time." (The answer key is found at the end of the session.)

---------------------UNDERSTAND THE STORY---------------------

As you read Chapter 28 of *The Story* during the week, allow the story of the beginning of the early church to help you see God's original plan for the church.

1. Why do you think God chose such a spectacular start for the church at Pentecost?

    _____

    _____

    _____

    _____

    _____

2. How do you explain the boldness of Peter and the disciples — the same men who abandoned Jesus in Gethsemane and denied him in the temple courts?

    _____

    _____

    _____

    _____

    _____

3. Based on what happened to Stephen, what do you think you would have felt and done when placed in the situation Ananias faced?

    _____

    _____

    _____

    _____

    _____

4. How do you explain why James was put to death but Peter was rescued from prison?

    _____

    _____

    _____

    _____

5. After reading Chapter 28, what is one question you wish you could ask God about what you have read?

_____

_____

_____

_____

_____

———————————LIVE THE STORY———————————

TAKE ACTION

We don't want to simply be hearers of the Word but also doers of the Word. Take some time to reflect on what you have read and studied this week.

1. Did you have a new discovery from your reading and study this week? If so, what was it?

_____

_____

_____

_____

2. Is there something you need to do based on what you learned?

_____

_____

_____

_____

3. Who can you tell about what you learned? Make a plan right now to share with that person.

_____

_____

_____

_____

TELL THE STORY

As we have gone through *The Story* together, we have been learning how to tell the story. This week we review Movement 3. Read Movement 3 below several times to make sure you have it committed to memory.

 ## Movement 3: The Story of Jesus (Matthew–John)

Jesus left the Upper Story to come down into our Lower Story to be with us and to provide the way for us to be made right with God. Through faith in Christ's work on the cross, we can now overturn Adam's choice and have a personal relationship with God.

CONVERSATION

One day around a meal or your dinner table, have an intentional conversation about this week's topic. During the meal, read John 14:25–27 found at the beginning of this session. Use the following question for discussion:

> What do you think the Holy Spirit wants to do in our lives each day?

PRAY TOGETHER

Focusing the last thoughts of our day on God can help us rest — truly rest — in him. Each night read and reflect on John 14:25–27, either on your own or with others if there are others living in your home. Pray and ask God to help you fully embrace the story of the rapid expansion of the early church. As you do this each night before bed, let the power of the verses impact both heart and mind.

● ● ●

Group Time

Welcome

Welcome to Session 28 of *The Story*. If there are any new members in your group, take time for introductions. You might open with a brief prayer asking God to help you understand and embrace the story of the exciting start of the early church.

KNOW THE STORY

Use one or both of these questions before you watch the video together.

1. How did you do on the quiz in the Know the Story section before you read the chapter?

2. What was your most interesting insight or question from your Personal Time this week?

UNDERSTAND THE STORY

As you watch the video for Session 28 of The Story, *use the section below to record some of the main points. (The answer key is found at the end of the session.)*

- The rest of the Bible tells of God's _____ pursuit of us.

- Now it's time for a new _____ with a new mission.

- The 120 disciples wait patiently in the upper room for the _____ to come.

- Everyone was filled with _____.

- This is where our lives intersect with the _____ Story.

LIVE THE STORY

TAKE ACTION

1. What part of Randy's teaching encouraged or challenged you the most? Why?

    _____

    _____

    _____

2. Did anything from your Personal Time jump out, calling you to action? Did anyone have an "aha" moment?

    _____

    _____

    _____

CONVERSATION

Have someone in your group read aloud the Case Study below and then discuss the questions that follow.

Kelly said, "I'm sorry, Wade. I just can't believe those stories of miracles from the Bible." Wade had an internal debate before he shared his story. "Kelly, last year I went on a mission trip to a rural place in Central America. We were building a church building for a local church. We were a four-hour bus ride from the closest city. One of the locals fell off the roof and broke his leg. I heard it break. I saw it bent off at a crazy angle. The local pastor said we couldn't take him into the city because they couldn't afford the doctors, so he was going to ask God to heal him. I started to offer to pay for the doctor, but the guy was in agony. A four-hour bus trip would be torture. The pastor knelt down, prayed for the Father to heal him, picked his leg up in his hands, and straightened it out right there. Ten minutes later, the local man from the church was walking around the job site."

1. Why do you think Wade debated before he shared his story?

2. Based on what you read and learned this week, how do you think Kelly will respond?

TELL THE STORY

As we have gone through *The Story* together, we have been learning each week how to tell the story. This week we review Movement 3. Read it aloud together to make sure you have it committed to memory. Repeat it until the group is able to say it without looking.

 Movement 3: The Story of Jesus (Matthew–John)

Jesus left the Upper Story to come down into our Lower Story to be with us and to provide the way for us to be made right with God. Through faith in Christ's work on the cross, we can now overturn Adam's choice and have a personal relationship with God.

PRAY TOGETHER

One of the most important things we can do together in community is to pray for each other and those around us. Review your prayer requests from last week, and look for ways God has answered the prayers of your group. Then use the space below to record prayer requests and praises for this week. Also, make sure to pray by name for people God might add to your group — especially your neighbors.

Name   *Request/Praise*

_____   _____

_____   _____

_____   _____

_____   _____

NEXT WEEK

Next week we'll look at the story of Paul's missionary journeys and how God expanded the church far beyond the borders of Israel.

Know the Story Answer Key — d / a / b / c

Video Notes Answer Key — relentless / community / Holy Spirit / awe / Upper

Paul's Mission

"I always thank my God for you because
of his grace given you in Christ Jesus. For
in him you have been enriched in every
way — with all kinds of speech and with
all knowledge — God thus confirming our
testimony about Christ among you."

1 CORINTHIANS 1:4 – 6

Paul's 1st missionary journey	Jerusalem Council	Paul's 2nd missionary journey	Paul's 3rd missionary journey
AD 46–48	49–50	50–52	53–57

Personal Time

Last week we looked at the story of the beginning of the early church. Perhaps you were amazed at all the ways God used miracles to advance his church.

This week before your Group Time and your weekend worship experience, spend time using the Personal Time section of your study guide to allow the story of Paul's missionary journeys to take root in your heart.

---KNOW THE STORY---

Before reading Chapter 29 of *The Story*, answer the questions below to test your knowledge of this week's Scripture. Enter your answers in the column marked "1st Time."

Question	1st Time	2nd Time
1		
2		
3		
4		

1. When Barnabas and Paul performed a miracle at Iconium, what did the crowds call them?
    a. They called them demon possessed.
    b. They called them sons of God.
    c. They called them Zeus and Hermes.
    d. They called them angels of light.

2. Why did the crowd oppose Paul in Ephesus?
    a. They rejected his message as narrow and foolish.
    b. They saw how following Paul's message was not good for trade.
    c. They felt they needed to defend their god, Zeus.
    d. Paul had condemned their pagan practices.

3. What does Paul say we are if we lack love?
    a. We are advocates for the enemy.
    b. We are worthless fools.
    c. We are wineskins with holes.
    d. We are resounding gongs.

4. Which city did not receive a letter from Paul?
    a. Athens
    b. Corinth
    c. Ephesus
    d. Thessalonica

Now read Chapter 29 of *The Story*. After reading, revisit the questions to check your answers. Put your new answers in the column marked "2nd Time." (The answer key is found at the end of the session.)

—————————UNDERSTAND THE STORY—————————

As you read Chapter 29 of *The Story* during the week, allow the story of Paul's missionary journeys to inspire you to live out your faith in your neighborhood and workplace.

1. What do you think provided the greatest encouragement to Paul to continue his missionary journeys?

2. Of all the opposition Paul faced, which seems to be the most difficult to you, and why?

3. How does knowing Paul had visited each of these cities affect the way you read his letters?

4. Of all the counsel he gives to the different churches, which piece of counsel challenges you most? Why?

5. After reading Chapter 29, what is one question you wish you could ask God about what you have read?

_____

_____

_____

_____

_____

—————————————LIVE THE STORY—————————————

TAKE ACTION

We don't want to simply be hearers of the Word but also doers of the Word. Take some time to reflect on what you have read and studied this week.

1. Did you have a new discovery from your reading and study this week? If so, what was it?

_____

_____

_____

_____

2. Is there something you need to do based on what you learned?

_____

_____

_____

_____

3. Who can you tell about what you learned? Make a plan right now to share with that person.

_____

_____

_____

_____

---TELL THE STORY---

As we have gone through *The Story* together, we have been learning how to tell the story. This week we review Movement 4. Read through Movement 4 below several times to make sure you have it committed to memory.

Movement 4: The Story of the Church (Acts–Jude)

Everyone who comes into a relationship with God through faith in Christ belongs to the new community God is building called the church. The church is commissioned to be the presence of Christ in the Lower Story — telling his story by the way we live and the words we speak. Every story of the church points people to the second coming of Christ, when he will return to restore God's original vision.

CONVERSATION

One day around a meal or your dinner table, have an intentional conversation about this week's topic. During the meal, read 1 Corinthians 1:4 – 6 found at the beginning of this session. Use the following questions for discussion:

> What do you think the word "enrich" means? What do you think God has done to enrich us?

PRAY TOGETHER

Focusing the last thoughts of our day on God can help us rest — truly rest — in him. Each night read and reflect on 1 Corinthians 1:4 – 6, either on your own or with others if there are others living in your home. Pray and ask God to help you fully embrace the powerful stories of Paul's various journeys. As you do this each night before bed, let the power of the verses impact both heart and mind.

● ● ●

Group Time

Welcome

Welcome to Session 29 of *The Story*. If there are any new members in your group, take time for introductions. You might open with a brief prayer asking God to help you understand and embrace the stories of Paul's missionary journeys.

KNOW THE STORY

Use one or both of these questions before you watch the video together.

1. How did you do on the quiz in the Know the Story section before you read the chapter?

   _____

   _____

   _____

2. What was your most interesting insight or question from your Personal Time this week?

   _____

   _____

   _____

UNDERSTAND THE STORY

As you watch the video for Session 29 of The Story, *use the section below to record some of the main points. (The answer key is found at the end of the session.)*

- Paul was eventually _____ for his work.

- Paul's home base is a place called _____.

- He offers up _____ to anyone who believes.

- Paul is _____ his life to the Upper Story of God.

- In this way the word of the Lord spread widely and grew in
  _____.

- The gospel has come to us because Paul was _____.

LIVE THE STORY

TAKE ACTION

1. What part of Randy's teaching encouraged or challenged you the most? Why?

_____

_____

_____

2. Did anything from your Personal Time jump out, calling you to action? Did anyone have an "aha" moment?

_____

_____

_____

CONVERSATION

Use one or two of the questions below (depending on time) to have a conversation in community.

1. How do the hardships and opposition Paul faced in each city challenge you in your faith?

_____

_____

_____

2. As you look at the various pieces of counsel Paul gave to the church, which ones have the greatest impact on you? Why?

_____

_____

_____

3. How did God use these journeys and the letters that followed to build up his church in the first century? How does he continue to use them today?

4. As you reflect on what you learned this week in Chapter 29, what is your biggest takeaway?

TELL THE STORY

As we have gone through *The Story* together, we have been learning each week how to tell the story. This week we review Movement 4. Read it aloud together to make sure you have it committed to memory. Repeat it until the group is able to say it without looking

∞ Movement 4: The Story of the Church (Acts–Jude)

Everyone who comes into a relationship with God through faith in Christ belongs to the new community God is building called the church. The church is commissioned to be the presence of Christ in the Lower Story — telling his story by the way we live and the words we speak. Every story of the church points people to the second coming of Christ, when he will return to restore God's original vision.

PRAY TOGETHER

One of the most important things we can do together in community is to pray for each other and those around us. Review your prayer requests from last week, and look for ways God has answered the prayers of your group. Then, use the space below to record prayer requests and praises for this week. Also, make sure to pray by name for people God might add to your group — especially your neighbors.

Name   *Request/Praise*

_____   _____

_____   _____

_____   _____

_____   _____

NEXT WEEK

Next week we'll look at the story of Paul's final days and how God worked mightily through him all the way to the end of his life.

Know the Story Answer Key — c / b / d / a

Video Notes Answer Key — beheaded / Antioch / salvation / aligning / power / obedient

Paul's Final Days

"And we know that in all things God works for the good of those who love him, who have been called according to his purpose."

ROMANS 8:28

Paul's 1st imprisonment in Rome	Paul's 2nd imprisonment and execution	John exiled on Patmos
59–62	67–68	90–95

AD

Personal Time

Last week we looked at the story of Paul's missionary journeys. Perhaps you were challenged by the words Paul had for the churches or the commitment Paul had to spread the gospel message.

This week before your Group Time and your weekend worship experience, spend time using the Personal Time section of your study guide to allow the story of Paul's final days in Rome to take root in your heart.

─────────── **KNOW THE STORY** ───────────

Before reading Chapter 30 of *The Story*, answer the questions below to test
your knowledge of this week's Scripture. Enter your answers in the column
marked "1st Time."

Question	1st Time	2nd Time
1		
2		
3		
4		

1. Why was the commander worried about the chains they had placed on Paul?
   a. Paul had not received a fair trial.
   b. The commander was afraid the crowd would attack and kill Paul.
   c. The commander found out Paul was a Roman citizen.
   d. Paul had broken out of similar chains in the past.

2. What happened to Paul right after he was shipwrecked on his journey?
   a. A poisonous snake bit him.
   b. He became violently ill from food he ate on the island.
   c. The centurion flogged him for preaching to the islanders.
   d. He managed to escape captivity and continued to preach in freedom.

3. Which of the following was not a phrase said by Paul to the church in
   Ephesus?
   a. For we are God's handiwork.
   b. You may be filled to the measure of all the fullness of God.
   c. Submit to one another out of reverence for Christ.
   d. All things are possible through unity in faith.

4. What did Paul tell Timothy would happen to everyone who wants to live
   a godly life in Christ Jesus?
   a. They will be blessed richly.
   b. They will be persecuted.
   c. They will be rewarded in the life to come.
   d. Family and friends will scorn them.

Now read Chapter 30 of *The Story*. After reading, revisit the questions to
check your answers. Put your new answers in the column marked "2nd Time."
(The answer key is found at the end of the session.)

UNDERSTAND THE STORY

As you read Chapter 30 of *The Story* during the week, allow the story of Paul's final missionary journey and his words to Timothy to help you focus your heart around God's Upper Story plans for your life.

1. Why do you think Paul faced such opposition from the crowds everywhere he went?

2. How does Paul's interaction with the elders from Ephesus shape (or reshape) your view of the apostle Paul?

3. What words to the church in Ephesus challenge you or encourage you the most, and why?

4. What words to Timothy challenge you or encourage you the most, and why?

5. After reading Chapter 30, what is one question you wish you could ask God about what you have read?

_____

_____

_____

_____

LIVE THE STORY

TAKE ACTION

We don't want to simply be hearers of the Word but also doers of the Word. Take some time to reflect on what you have read and studied this week.

1. Did you have a new discovery from your reading and study this week? If so, what was it?

_____

_____

_____

_____

2. Is there something you need to do based on what you learned?

_____

_____

_____

_____

3. Who can you tell about what you learned? Make a plan right now to share with that person.

_____

_____

_____

_____

TELL THE STORY

As we have gone through *The Story* together, we have been learning how to tell the story. This week we review Movement 5. Read through Movement 5 below several times to make sure you have it committed to memory.

🌀 Movement 5: The Story of a New Garden (Revelation)

God will one day create a new earth and a new garden and once again come down to be with us. All who placed their faith in Christ in this life will be eternal residents in the life to come.

CONVERSATION

One day around a meal or your dinner table, have an intentional conversation about this week's topic. During the meal, read Romans 8:28 found at the beginning of this session. Use the following question for discussion:

> What ways does God work things out for our good—even things that are difficult?

PRAY TOGETHER

Focusing the last thoughts of our day on God can help us rest — truly rest — in him. Each night read and reflect on Romans 8:28, either on your own or with others if there are others living in your home. Pray and ask God to help you fully embrace the story of Paul's final days of ministry from Rome. As you do this each night before bed, let the power of the verse impact both heart and mind.

● ● ●

Group Time

Welcome

Welcome to Session 30 of *The Story*. If there are any new members in your group, take time for introductions. You might open with a brief prayer asking God to help you understand and embrace the story of Paul's final ministry days.

KNOW THE STORY

Use one or both of these questions before you watch the video together.

1. How did you do on the quiz in the Know the Story section before you read the chapter?

   _____

   _____

   _____

2. What was your most interesting insight or question from your Personal Time this week?

   _____

   _____

   _____

UNDERSTAND THE STORY

As you watch the video for Session 30 of The Story, *use the section below to record some of the main points. (The answer key is found at the end of the session.)*

- Our mission is to conform to the _____ of Christ for the sake of others.

- The whole body grows and builds itself up in _____.

- "For this reason I remind you to fan into _____ the gift of God."

- "I have fought the good fight. I have finished the _____. I have kept the faith."
- We need to individually and _____ align our lives to the Upper Story of God.

LIVE THE STORY

TAKE ACTION

1. What part of Randy's teaching encouraged or challenged you the most? Why?

    _____

    _____

    _____

2. Did anything from your Personal Time jump out, to you calling you to action? Did anyone have an "aha" moment?

    _____

    _____

    _____

CONVERSATION

Have someone in your group read aloud the Case Study below and then discuss the questions that follow.

Miss Grace had lived in the neighborhood for over fifty years, and everyone knew her. Her husband, Charlie, had passed away twenty years earlier. Miss Grace was a pillar in the community. While several neighbors came alongside Miss Grace to help with yard work or check on her, the entire neighborhood was truly the beneficiary of her wisdom and words. Bonnie had spent Tuesday mornings for the last two years having coffee for an hour with Miss Grace. Yesterday morning, Miss Grace had looked deeply into Bonnie's eyes and said, "I pray God would chisel away everything in your life that doesn't look like Jesus." For the last twenty-four hours, Bonnie had wrestled with these words wondering how to apply them.

1. How have you had older and wiser people speak into your life in the past? How are you pursuing this type of interaction in your life today?

2. Based on what you read and learned this week about Paul (including his words to Timothy), how would you encourage Bonnie to respond to what Miss Grace shared with her?

TELL THE STORY

As we have gone through *The Story* together, we have been learning together each week how to tell the story. This week we review Movement 5. Read it aloud together to make sure you have it committed to memory. Repeat it until the group is able to say it without looking.

Movement 5: The Story of a New Garden (Revelation)

God will one day create a new earth and a new garden and once again come down to be with us. All who placed their faith in Christ in this life will be eternal residents in the life to come.

PRAY TOGETHER

One of the most important things we can do together in community is to pray for each other and those around us. Review your prayer requests from last week, and look for ways God has answered the prayers of your group. Then use the space below to record prayer requests and praises for this week. Also, make sure to pray by name for people God might add to your group — especially your neighbors.

Name   *Request/Praise*

_____   _____

_____   _____

_____   _____

NEXT WEEK

Next week we'll look at the final words of John through the revelation and how those words bring the Upper Story full circle.

Know the Story Answer Key — c / a / d / b

Video Notes Answer Key — image / love / flame / race / collectively

The End of Time

"These words are trustworthy and true. The
Lord, the God who inspires the prophets,
sent his angel to show his servants the
things that must soon take place."

REVELATION 22:6

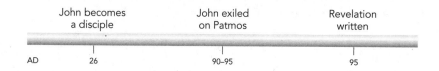

	John becomes a disciple	John exiled on Patmos	Revelation written
AD	26	90–95	95

Personal Time

Last week we looked at the stories of Paul's final days and his words to the
church. Perhaps you were encouraged by the example of Paul.

This week before your Group Time and your weekend worship experience,
spend time using the Personal Time section of your study guide to allow the
story of God's coming promises to take root in your heart.

KNOW THE STORY

Before reading Chapter 31 of *The Story*, answer the questions below to test your knowledge of this week's Scripture. Enter your answers in the column marked "1st Time."

Question	1st Time	2nd Time
1		
2		
3		
4		

1. How many churches were involved in the vision John was given by Jesus?
   a. Three
   b. Five
   c. Seven
   d. Twelve

2. What was in the right hand of the one who sat on the throne?
   a. A scepter
   b. A scroll
   c. A crown
   d. A book

3. What name was written on the robe and thigh of the rider of the white horse?
   a. King of Kings and Lord of Lords
   b. Faithful and True
   c. Lamb of God
   d. Savior of the World

4. What will we eat in the New Jerusalem that was also in the original garden?
   a. Food from the banquet table of God
   b. The word from the scroll of God
   c. Unblemished fruits and vegetables
   d. Fruit from the tree of life

Now read Chapter 31 of *The Story*. After reading, revisit the questions to check your answers. Put your new answers in the column marked "2nd Time." (The answer key is found at the end of the session.)

UNDERSTAND THE STORY

As you read Chapter 31 of *The Story* during the week, allow the story of the revelation of John to help you see God's Upper Story plans for the future.

1. Which words of John to the churches do you find most challenging for the church in your current culture?

2. Imagine the vision John was receiving as he tried to write down what he saw. In a few sentences, describe the scene around the throne in your own words.

3. As Jesus returns in victory and judgment, what part of that raises the greatest concern for you? What part gives you the most hope?

4. In the description of the new heaven and the new earth, what part of that description is the most exciting to you? Why?

5. After reading Chapter 31, what is one question you wish you could ask God about what you have read?

_____

_____

_____

_____

LIVE THE STORY

TAKE ACTION

We don't want to simply be hearers of the Word but also doers of the Word. Take some time to reflect on what you have read and studied this week.

1. Did you have a new discovery from your reading and study this week? If so, what was it?

_____

_____

_____

_____

2. Is there something you need to do based on what you learned?

_____

_____

_____

_____

3. Who can you tell about what you learned? Make a plan right now to share with that person.

_____

_____

_____

_____

―――――――――――――――TELL THE STORY―――――――――――――

As we have gone through *The Story* together, we have learned how to tell the story. This week we will focus on all five movements. Read through each of the movements below several times as you make sure you have committed them to memory.

Movement 1: The Story of the Garden (Genesis 1–11)

In the Upper Story, God creates the Lower Story. His vision is to come down and be with us in a beautiful garden. The first two people reject God's vision and are escorted from paradise. Their decision introduces sin into the human race and keeps us from community with God. At this moment God gives a promise and launches a plan to get us back. The rest of the Bible is God's story of how he kept that promise and made it possible for us to enter a loving relationship with him.

Movement 2: The Story of Israel (Genesis 12–Malachi)

God builds a brand-new nation called Israel. Through this nation, he will reveal his presence, power, and plan to get us back. Every story of Israel will point to the first coming of Jesus — the One who will provide the way back to God.

Movement 3: The Story of Jesus (Matthew–John)

Jesus left the Upper Story to come down into our Lower Story to be with us and to provide the way for us to be made right with God. Through faith in Christ's work on the cross, we can now overturn Adam's choice and have a personal relationship with God.

Movement 4: The Story of the Church (Acts–Jude)

Everyone who comes into a relationship with God through faith in Christ belongs to the new community God is building called the church. The church is commissioned to be the presence of Christ in the Lower Story — telling his story by the way we live and the words we speak. Every story of the church points people to the second coming of Christ, when he will return to restore God's original vision.

🌳 Movement 5: The Story of a New Garden (Revelation)

God will one day create a new earth and a new garden and once again come down to be with us. All who placed their faith in Christ in this life will be eternal residents in the life to come.

CONVERSATION

One day around a meal or your dinner table, have an intentional conversation about this week's topic. During the meal, read Revelation 22:6 found at the beginning of this session. Use the following question for discussion:

> Why do you think God might sometimes use angels to communicate with us?

PRAY TOGETHER

Focusing the last thoughts of our day on God can help us rest — truly rest — in him. Each night read and reflect on Revelation 22:6, either on your own or with others if there are others living in your home. Pray and ask God to help you fully embrace the story of his future for his chosen people. As you do this each night before bed, let the power of the verse impact both heart and mind.

● ● ●

Group Time

Welcome

Welcome to Session 31 of *The Story*. If there are any new members in your group, take time for introductions. You might open with a brief prayer asking God to help you understand and embrace the story of his planned future for the end of time.

KNOW THE STORY

Use one or both of these questions before you watch the video together.

1. How did you do on the quiz in the Know the Story section before you read the chapter?

   _____

   _____

   _____

2. What was your most interesting insight or question from your Personal Time this week?

   _____

   _____

   _____

UNDERSTAND THE STORY

As you watch the video for Session 31 of The Story, *use the section below to record some of the main points. (The answer key is found at the end of the session.)*

- His name will be on their _____.
- "Then I saw a new heaven and a new _____."
- He will wipe every _____ from their eyes.
- "I am the _____ and the _____."

- There are _____ of life.
- God's _____ Story vision is completely restored.

────────────────── LIVE THE STORY ──────────────────

TAKE ACTION

1. What part of Randy's teaching encouraged or challenged you the most? Why?

2. Did anything from your Personal Time jump out, calling you to action? Did anyone have an "aha" moment?

CONVERSATION

Use one or two of the questions below (depending on time) to have a conversation in community.

1. How did learning to tell the story impact your view and understanding of God?

2. What is the greatest challenge to you in John's words to the seven churches?

3. What is the one thing you are looking forward to most in the new heaven and the new earth based on John's description? Did anything surprise you?

4. As you reflect on what you learned this week in Chapter 31, what is your biggest takeaway?

_____

_____

_____

TELL THE STORY

As we have gone through *The Story* together, we have learned how to tell the story. This week we will focus on all five movements. Read each of them aloud as you make sure you have committed them to memory. See if you can recite them as a group without looking.

🌳 Movement 1: The Story of the Garden (Genesis 1–11)

In the Upper Story, God creates the Lower Story. His vision is to come down and be with us in a beautiful garden. The first two people reject God's vision and are escorted from paradise. Their decision introduces sin into the human race and keeps us from community with God. At this moment God gives a promise and launches a plan to get us back. The rest of the Bible is God's story of how he kept that promise and made it possible for us to enter a loving relationship with him.

🕎 Movement 2: The Story of Israel (Genesis 12–Malachi)

God builds a brand-new nation called Israel. Through this nation, he will reveal his presence, power, and plan to get us back. Every story of Israel will point to the first coming of Jesus — the One who will provide the way back to God.

✝ Movement 3: The Story of Jesus (Matthew–John)

Jesus left the Upper Story to come down into our Lower Story to be with us and to provide the way for us to be made right with God. Through faith in Christ's work on the cross, we can now overturn Adam's choice and have a personal relationship with God.

Movement 4: The Story of the Church (Acts–Jude)

Everyone who comes into a relationship with God through faith in Christ belongs to the new community God is building called the church. The church is commissioned to be the presence of Christ in the Lower Story—telling his story by the way we live and the words we speak. Every story of the church points people to the second coming of Christ, when he will return to restore God's original vision.

Movement 5: The Story of a New Garden (Revelation)

God will one day create a new earth and a new garden and once again come down to be with us. All who placed their faith in Christ in this life will be eternal residents in the life to come.

PRAY TOGETHER

One of the most important things we can do together in community is to pray for each other and those around us. Review your prayer requests from last week, and look for ways God has answered the prayers of your group. Then use the space below to record prayer requests and praises for this week. Also, make sure to pray by name for people God might add to your group—especially your neighbors.

Name   *Request/Praise*

_____   _____

_____   _____

_____   _____

_____

Know the Story Answer Key—c / b / a / d

Video Notes Answer Key—foreheads / earth / tear / Alpha / Omega / trees / Upper

THE STORY

POWERED BY **ZONDERVAN**

READ THE STORY. EXPERIENCE THE BIBLE.

Here I am, 50 years old. I have been to college, seminary, engaged in ministry my whole life, my dad is in ministry, my grandfather was in ministry, and *The Story* **has been one of the most unique experiences of my life.** The Bible has been made fresh for me. It has made God's redemptive plan come alive for me once again.
—Seth Buckley, Youth Pastor, Spartanburg Baptist Church, Spartanburg, SC

As my family and I went through *The Story* together, the more I began to believe and the more real [the Bible] became to me, and **it rubbed off on my children and helped them with their walk with the Lord.** *The Story* inspired conversations we might not normally have had.
—Kelly Leonard, Parent, Shepherd of the Hills Christian Church, Porter Ranch, CA

We have people reading *The Story*—**some devour it and can't wait for the next week.** Some have never really read the Bible much, so it's exciting to see a lot of adults reading the Word of God for the first time. I've heard wonderful things from people who are long-time readers of Scripture. They're excited about how it's all being tied together for them. It just seems to make more sense.

—Lynnette Schulz, Director of Worship Peace Lutheran Church, Eau Claire, WI

FOR ADULTS

9780310950974

FOR STUDENTS

9780310759829

FOR KIDS

9780310759645

TheStory.com

Dive into the Bible in a whole new way!

The Story is changing lives, making it easy for any person, regardless of age or biblical literacy level, to understand the Bible.

The Story comes in five editions, one for each age group from toddlers to adults. All five editions are organized chronologically into 31 chapters with selected Scripture from Genesis to Revelation. The additional resources create an engaging group Bible-reading experience, whether you read *The Story* with your whole church, in small groups, or with your family.

- **Adults** – Read the Bible as one compelling story, from Genesis to Revelation. Available in NIV, KJV, NKJV, large print, and audio editions. Curriculum DVD and Study Guide also available.

- **Students** – Student edition of *The Story*, with special study helps and features designed with students in mind. Curriculum DVD also available.

- **Children** – With a Kids' Edition for ages 8-12, a Storybook Bible for ages 4-8, a Storybook Bible for toddlers, fun trading cards, and four levels of curriculum for twos, preschool, early elementary, and later elementary, children of all ages will learn how their story fits into God's story.

- **Churches** – *The Story* is flexible, affordable, and easy to use with your church, in any ministry, from nursery to adult Sunday school, small groups to youth group…and even the whole church.

- **Spanish** – *The Story* resources are also available in Spanish.

FOR CHILDREN

FOR CHURCHES

9780310719755

9780310719274

Church Kit   9780310941538

THE STORY

POWERED BY ZONDERVAN

BELIEVE

POWERED BY ZONDERVAN

Dear Reader,

Notable researcher George Gallup Jr. summarized his findings on the state of American Christianity with this startling revelation: "Churches face no greater challenge...than overcoming biblical illiteracy, and the prospects for doing so are formidable because **the stark fact is, many Christians don't know what they believe or why.**"

The problem is not that people lack a hunger for God's Word. Research tells us that the number one thing people want from their church is for it to help them understand the Bible, and that Bible engagement is the number one catalyst for spiritual growth. Nothing else comes close.

This is why I am passionate about the book you're holding in your hands: *Believe*— a Bible engagement experience to anchor every member of your family in the key teachings of Scripture.

The *Believe* experience helps you answer three significant questions: Can you clearly articulate the essentials of the faith? Would your neighbors or coworkers identify you as a Christian based on their interactions with you and your family? Is the kingdom of God expanding in your corner of the world?

Grounded in Scripture, *Believe* is a spiritual growth experience for all ages, taking each person on a journey toward becoming more like Jesus in their beliefs, actions, and character. There is one edition for adults, one for students, and two versions for children. All four age-appropriate editions of *Believe* unpack the 10 key beliefs, 10 key practices, and 10 key virtues of a Christian, so that everyone in your family and your church can learn together to be more like Jesus.

When these timeless truths are understood, believed in the heart, and applied to our daily living, they will transform a life, a family, a church, a city, a nation, and even our world.

Imagine thousands of churches and hundreds of thousands of individuals all over the world who will finally be able to declare – **"I know what I believe and why, and in God's strength I will seek to live it out all the days of my life."** It could change the world. It has in the past; it could happen again.

In Him,

Randy Frazee
General Editor, *Believe*

LIVING THE STORY OF THE BIBLE TO BECOME LIKE JESUS

Teach your whole family how to live the story of the Bible!

- **Adults** – Unlocks the 10 key beliefs, 10 key practices, and 10 key virtues that help people live the story of the Bible. Curriculum DVD and Study Guide also available.

- ***Think, Act, Be Like Jesus*** – A companion to *Believe*, this fresh resource by pastor Randy Frazee will help readers develop a personal vision for spiritual growth and a simple plan for getting started on the *Believe* journey.

- **Students** – Student edition of *Believe* with study questions and fun features to engage teens and students. Curriculum DVD also available.

- **Children** – With a Kids' Edition for ages 8-12, a Storybook for ages 4-8, a coloring book for toddlers, and four levels of curriculum for twos, preschool, early elementary, and later elementary, children of all ages will learn how to think, act, and be like Jesus.

- **Churches** – *Believe* is flexible, affordable, and easy to use with your church, in any ministry, from nursery to adult Sunday school, small groups to youth group…and even the whole church.

- **Spanish** – All *Believe* resources are also available in Spanish.

FOR ADULTS

9780310443834

9780310250173

FOR STUDENTS

9780310745617

FOR CHILDREN

9780310746010

9780310745907

9780310752226

FOR CHURCHES

Church Kit 9780310681717

BelieveTheStory.com

BELIEVE
POWERED BY ZONDERVAN

THE STORY DEVOTIONAL
Discover Your Role in God's Story

See your life and purpose in a whole new light—as part of God's epic story—with this beautiful devotional. Through 365 daily Scripture readings arranged chronologically, plus bite-sized reflections and a daily takeaway, this unique devotional illuminates how God has been weaving his plan throughout history. Each day, you'll be blessed with a reminder of God's unrelenting love and pursuit of his people.

Softcover   9780310084754